Don't
Skate
on the
Piano

Ann Daly Goodwin

For the 13 who came
For the original three
Nancy, Jack the Younger and Joan

and

For Jack the Elder
my partner in parenting
and everything else

Don't Skate on the Piano

The First Rule for Foster Families

Ann Daly Goodwin

Contents

Introduction

In "A Child's Christmas in Wales," a classic introduced to me by Ann Daly Goodwin, Dylan Thomas talks of reaching deep into the new-fallen December snow and pulling out an assortment of treasured memories.

Reading Ann's memoir of our tribe of 13 brings to mind that image. She slips back into our shared past and creates vignettes of fierce and boundless love.

I was outwardly the least needy of the 13 teens who boarded at Hotel Goodwin, yet the impact of Ann and Jack on my life has been profound.

I was interested in writing for my high school paper. She as my journalism teacher and Jack as a career journalist were largely responsible for firing that interest into a vocational passion that carried me to a 40-plus year career as a reporter at the *Star Tribune* in Minneapolis. Beyond that, Ann's stories of her days marching in Selma inspired my still-forming social conscience. Her deep commitment to human rights taught me the compassion for the underdog that undergirds the best journalism. Most of all, the limitless compassion she and Jack shared for the people who entered their lives taught me the power of love as a transforming force.

Make no mistake. Ann and Jack Goodwin were a team, adding up to more than the sum of their parts. What they accomplished as a couple could not have been accomplished individually. Their implicit faith in each other and seemingly seamless backstopping of one another appeared more effortless than I'm sure it was. Jack worked an early-morning shift and kept the domestic side on track as their ever-expanding brood returned from school. Ann's daytime teaching shift was followed by long evenings preparing for the next day's meals atop correcting an endless supply of student papers.

Ann and Jack met as students while working on the newspaper of their alma mater, Carleton College. Jack then went to work for the Minneapolis newspapers and stayed there for 41 years, anchoring often-chaotic newsrooms with his unruffled professionalism. Ann, after starting married life in the baby-birthing, toddler-raising mold, entered the work force in the 1960s. She worked for a suburban newspaper, earned her master's degree, taught high school and college journalism and capped her career as an editorial and column writer for the St. Paul *Pioneer Press*, earning several national honors for her work.

Read this book and you will be immersed in a world where limitless empathy combined with tough love to mold lives.

—Steve Brandt

Preface

WE DIDN'T PLAN IT that way. We didn't plan a 10-year roll-er-coaster ride when my husband and I would be foster parents for 13 youngsters, many of them from abusive, dysfunctional families. It just happened, kid by kid.

That foster-care decade was a challenge. During that space, we felt some pain and much exhilaration, a number of lows and multiple highs.

More calls for help came than our family could answer. "Yes" or "no" was always a family decision. Turn-downs made us somber, because we knew teens in trouble faced a severe shortage of possible foster homes.

They still do.

With the exception of Steve Brandt, names of our foster children have been changed to protect their privacy and that of their families.

1.

The Stork as Superbird

SOME PEOPLE'S CHILDREN BRING home puppies. Our kids brought home kids.

That accounts for how the tally of young people in our household fluctuated as some youngsters left—usually after high-school graduation—and others came. When the last one launched out on her own, my husband and I had been father and mother to 16.

Thirteen of them are white, three are black and two of them married each other. Twice, seven were in residence at once, most of them clustered between the ages of 14 and 16.

How to describe our household in a single word? Lively.

The stork assigned to our house delivered some bundles weighing 100 pounds and more. The hefty bird began doing extra duty when our original, biological three were in their teens. Her initial aide was our son, Jack the Younger, who clattered up from his downstairs bedroom one morning with an announcement.

"I have a friend who wants to live with us," he said. And up popped David, having gained our boy's attention with a rain of pebbles against the proper windowpane around 3 a.m.

We knew the boy well. He and our son had met at church camp one summer and cemented their friendship the next.

We said, "David, it isn't possible. We like you to visit, but you already have a home."

We knew little about that home, but there was trouble there, so David's probation officer came to check us out. Did we see ourselves as riding to the rescue without a clue of what we were getting into? Or did we know and care about this young boy?

Not knowing what we were getting into—that part was right. But so was the part about knowing and caring.

Next came an interval of paperwork, questions and inspections. We didn't have so much as a parking ticket. We did have two exits from the lower level, where the boys would be sleeping. And so it went.

We passed muster. It was official. We were a foster family.

On his first night with us, black David from the inner city went off to play-practice with his new brother, to a sprawling, nearly all-white suburban school where he knew not a single other student.

The probation officer told us, "If he makes it with you for a month, he's made it." David made it for five years, our longest foster-teen resident of all.

"I have this friend and he has this problem....." That got to be a litany from Jack the Younger, his sister Nancy or their sister Joan.

Next would come the parental response: "Yes, dear. When is he coming to live with us?"

Then the crucial question: "What's his type of underwear?" The newcomers ran heavily to boys; how could I sort the laundry if one more male favored jockeys?

This scene was repeated off and on for years as we became family to a minor tide of teens.

Two of them simply needed a place to park while they finished high school with their pals; it's wrenching when your parents must move to a distant state just as you are launching into your senior year. Some needed time and space away when upheavals with sorely tried mothers and fathers got out of hand. Others limped in, gashed on the jagged edges of their ailing families.

Like that pebble-pitching first arrival, most of the youngsters who emerged from our lower level, or turned up at our table, were our children's friends. Sometimes the teens themselves whistled down that stork for a berth with us. Sometimes adults did it for them. A minister, school counselor, social worker and probation officer all did their bit to fill our beds. But Nancy, Jack and Joan were the chief suppliers.

One of my neighbors commented that everybody she knew had a family doctor. Some had a family lawyer. But we were the only ones in her circle of friends who could claim a family probation officer.

Here's one way probation can bring a child to foster care: Pretend you are a wounded kid, often truant from school—that's how you got on probation in the first place. Pretend you turn from the turmoil wracking your family and whisper to your social worker, "How do I get out?"

That's what Roger did, David's younger brother.

The social worker looked at the ceiling, out the window, anywhere but at Roger, and mumbled something noncommittal. He could not in good conscience tell the truth: The road out for Roger was to get himself in deeper trouble.

So the boy figured it out. He stole a car.

The day after that, he came to live with us. He stayed a long time, three years in fact, until things settled down back in his birth home.

Car theft made for a dramatic arrival, but there were others as stirring. Laura, our youngest daughter's dearest friend, hid behind the pine tree in our front yard for an hour on a frigid January night, working up the courage to ring our bell and tell us she'd left home.

Laura had lived first with her mother after her parents divorced, then with her father in the South, then back in Minnesota with her mother again.

Nobody seemed to have much time for her. Finally. Somebody. Did.

She was 15 years old. She was pregnant.

She made the abortion decision. She could not do it.

She made the adoption decision. She could not do it.

But stay in high school? She could and she would.

So Alan was born, and he and Laura went home from the hospital to Laura's mother, there to live until the teen-age student/parent could earn her diploma.

But Laura's mom was too fragile for the stress of a baby. Hence came Laura out of the night, infant in her arms, trudging four blocks to our house and hesitating behind that shielding tree. Finally, when the gentle snow picked up and the wind began to whistle, she swept inside like the buffeted heroine in some Victorian novel.

Another of our girls, Cathy, walked from the suburb where she lived to a juvenile detention center in the city. She carried two things with her: a comb for her long, brown hair and a one-volume edition of Shakespeare's plays.

To the people at the detention center she said, "Lock me up and get me out."

Out of what?

By the time Cathy was 3 years old, her mother had come to believe that her child was demon-possessed. This thing she believed gave her daughter's siblings permission to humiliate and abuse her.

When Cathy was a high-school sophomore, she could bear it no longer and she escaped, not from a lock-up, but into one, on purpose.

I was teaching then and Cathy was my student. There were hearings before a juvenile court judge. There were circumstances revealed by a high-school counselor. And so it was that Cathy could leave her home and come to us.

The most unusual place from which one of our teenagers sprang was a Salvation Army drop-box. You know—one of those big bins where people deposit items they no longer need.

Daniel, our son's best buddy, had left home after a series of epic scenes. To go on living with his family, he was told, the lad would need to temper his liberal tongue. That he could not seem to do. So out he was cast. For several nights he disappeared into that big, hard box to sleep, rearranging whatever was there to make a kind of bed.

One day at school, Jack the Younger wheedled out of Daniel the cold turn his life had taken and relayed the news to our minister. I smile at the mental image of that good man knocking on the makeshift shelter that night and dangling the right words to entice Daniel out.

They came straight to our house. I saw the two of them coming up our walk on a shivery September night. I remember the weather because I had not yet moved my 5-foot ivy plant to its sunny winter quarters inside. Caught by a sudden frost warning, I dashed out through the garage, snatching tools as I went.

There I stood astride my front-step planter, hacking ineffectively around the ivy's robust roots with the biggest spade I could muster. I was clad in thick gloves, woolly scarf and long winter coat, my pink pajama legs peeking out from underneath. It was sometime after 11 p.m.

The clergyman appeared, Daniel trailing after him like some frost-prone vine. They stopped. They stared.

Said my bemused minister, "You are the only woman I know who gardens in the middle of the night." Happily, he planted the youngster with us anyway.

After Daniel came Patti.

We had known Patti since she was in kindergarten. With their last names close in spelling, she and our son Jack were forever in the same classes. I can't remember a time when she wasn't popping in and out.

Then came high school. She and Daniel fell in love. And we thought she had been at our house a lot before!

But there was more to it than that.

Patti was the middle child, with a sister on either side. Patti was supposed to be the boy. Patti seldom sensed the approval that her siblings seemed to earn so easily.

Patti didn't break laws, do drugs, get pregnant or go on the street.

But she did break house rules, one in particular. In a church-going family, she stopped attending services. As an example, she found herself in fundamental disagreement with ministers who preached that unbaptized babies go to hell.

Ultimately, she resolved to avoid places of worship altogether.

Patti has been to church only once since she left home. One of her sisters, more comfortable with their parents' religious convictions, had in time become a minister; Patti attended her newly-ordained sister's Christmas service years ago. As for the future, Patti has promised Jack and me that she will come to our funerals. Whatever it takes.....

So for more reasons than we knew at the time, Patti declared herself one of us, married Daniel and moved into the downstairs bedroom with him.

Another new arrival was entirely my fault. I met a former student for lunch one day. Our friendship had gotten off to a spectacular start, back when he was a high school junior and I his journalism teacher.

I had planned a "happening," as instructors in journalism are inclined to do. My co-conspirator was the school's assistant principal, who had agreed to help me stage a classroom drama. Our goal was to make our act seem real to the students, stopping short of scaring them.

I hadn't counted on such a convincing performance from the administrator, he of the booming voice and linebacker build. He strode unannounced into my classroom, waving a newly minted copy of the student newspaper, claiming misquotation and threatening mischief for the adviser—me.

He backed me against the blackboard. He accused me of incompetence, shook his fist under my nose and demanded my resignation.

Our script had called for me to face him down. I never got to do it.

Up from his seat rose Steve, a skinny kid, a biblical David, unable to restrain his indignation. He stoutly defended his teacher and then flung out his parting shot with stinging scorn: "No gentleman should speak to a lady like that!"

I tried to get back into the act.

"Please sit down, Steve; I can handle this."

For all the notice the two of them took, I might as well have been off in Judah, scribbling psalms.

"What's your name, young man?" the administrator demanded.

"Steven Brandt, sir."

"I'll see you in my office, Steven Brandt."

"I'll see you in your office anytime you say, sir."

For one frozen moment man and boy glared at one another. Then the man stalked out of the room, banging the door behind him.

It was the gutsiest thing I ever saw a student do.

Silence hung, thick as fog. How will teacher explain the little skit, the exercise in observation gone awry? How will administrator deal with bold student? How will bold student feel when deception is revealed?

Not to worry. Back came Goliath and seized the giant-killer's hand, beaming congratulations at the teenager who stood up to the "bully".

Steve became editor of his high school paper, managing editor of the University of Minnesota Daily and, in due time, a professional journalist. Not to mention former teacher's fast friend.

So it seemed the most natural thing in the world for Steve and me to be sharing lunch one day during his university years. He confided that he needed a place to stay for the summer, so I asked him to come and live with us.

Yes, it seemed the most natural thing in the world, rather like inquiring if I should pass him the salt and pepper. I never stopped to think that checking out the invitation with Jack the Elder after the fact would be awkward at best and possibly even unfair.

I went home and stumbled into it: "Guess which of my favorite students I saw today?"

Then (with some embarrassment), "His parents are moving, did you know?"

Then (with more embarrassment), "He's found a summer job at the university."

Then (with near-terminal embarrassment), "So it seemed logical....."

Actually it wasn't logical at all and I got stuck, "ummming" and "ahhhhing." I might be stuck there still, but for my husband's rescue.

He who knew me ever-so-well said ever-so-gently, "Ann, if you've asked Steve to come and live with us, it's all right with me." I detected the hint of a twinkle: The marriage was intact.

The degree of my discomfort and the extent of Jack's tolerance must be measured against the fact that our three-bedroom rambler was already bulging with six other teenagers, only three of whom bore our own last name.

It had reached the point where our letter carrier stopped asking, "Does this person live here too?" One day he said in mock despair, "If it's got your address, I deliver it."

So when Steve came he made seven, one of the two times when we decided we were at capacity. Needing to find space for another bed, we slipped a mattress under the stairs. That was a tad less dreary than it sounds; to give the teen sleeper something more inspiring to look at than the backside of steps, we tacked a midnight-blue cloth up there, studded with luminous stars.

Steve wasn't a speck of trouble, but inserting another teenager into the boys' dormitory on that lower level was like throwing a blob of butter into a saucepan of fudge and waiting to see if it boiled over.

That September, I staggered into the lounge at the high school where I taught.

"What did you do over the summer?" one of my colleagues asked.

"Survived," I said.

If you had been part of our family then, you would have known that the prized spot in that basement dorm was the bedroom at the end of it. Two windows let in plenty of light. The curtains and wallpaper were white, dashed with red. The roomy closet would be all yours. And when you'd had enough of the boiling fudge, there was the door to close.

Tania was lucky. By the time she came, she found no one in competition for the favored hideaway.

She came, but she almost didn't stay.

David the pebble-pitcher, our first, had wanted to come, had sat at our table several times, had already forged a friendship with Jack the Younger. But then we had teenagers like Tania, who were hauled from who-knew-what and plunked in the midst of people who played the family game by unfamiliar rules.

It was the foster kids who did the serious adjusting. We just shuffled beds around.

We knew very little about Tania – our last – only that her mother, who had repeatedly kept her daughter out of school to tend younger siblings, could no longer care for her children at all. Tania was placed in a group home, and her little brothers and sisters with foster families.

Tania was not so easy to place with a family, since she was a teen.

Her social worker heard that we were sheltering others her age. Given the path we were on, I suppose it was inevitable: Our two and a half years with Tania were about to begin.

Tania knew only that we were white folks from the suburbs. She must have been told more, but for a black kid from the inner city, it might have been all she heard.

She came for a trial weekend. The sensible rule was that at the end of that time, the social worker would take her away again for a few days, giving all parties a chance to think it over.

Jack and I thought we had come to the end of an era; 15 kids are enough for most families. But Tania wasn't in our house 10 minutes before we knew we wanted just one more—this one.

As for Tania, she was uneasy and on guard. Nobody her age was around for reassurance. She would be the caboose; all our other kids were out and on their own.

Things were not going well until Cathy dropped in for a visit. She took in the scene and whisked Tania away.

"We're going out for burgers," she said. "We'll be gone awhile."

We haven't a clue what the veteran said to put the tenderfoot at ease. Goodness only knows how many burgers it took. But when the two of them returned three hours later, Tania had made up her mind to try her luck with us.

As promised, the social worker came back on Sunday night to pick her up. Tania dug in her heels, but the sensible rule was the sensible rule. Off she must go for that think-it-over interval.

I can see her now, hanging out the window of the social worker's car. "Don't forget, I want the basement bedroom!" she hollered.

And in that room she soon settled. She nestled there for more than two years, until the time came for her to don a cap and gown, march across the stage and launch into the rest of her life.

As her graduation neared, I was bemoaning the fact that she was the end of our line.

The house would be so quiet. It would seem so empty.

"Honey," said my husband, "some people know how to stop having children."

He was right, of course.

2.

Spare the Piano

WE DIDN'T TIPTOE AROUND when teenagers came new to the family. We laid the rules on them right away:

1. No skating on the piano.

2. No snitching the last slice of lunch meat.

3. No dipping into containers marked "No! No!"—that meant the contents were earmarked for dinner. This rule provided us with our first glimpse of Cathy's wry sense of humor. When first she saw that sign, she tipped it upside-down so that it read "On! On!"

4. No driving off in an automobile without signing up for it first. This one helped keep the peace in a family with two cars and as many as six teen-age drivers, especially since one vehicle was reserved for the parents. Age does have certain privileges.

The teens only tended to forget this rule once, as the time Steve and Nancy made a theater date and walked out the door to find themselves without wheels. They got where they were going by curtain time only because fatherly compassion supplied the keys to the parental car.

The last-slice-of-lunch-meat law underscored two points: The father of the crew needed something saved for his brown bag, but everything else in the fridge was fair game.

When one of our boys first came, he never asked for snacks. Then when mealtime rolled around, he wolfed down so much, so fast, that we feared death by choking. We finally figured out that in his experience, you'd better eat all you could, as quickly as you could, while it was there in front of you; who knew when you might see food again?

That lad, and all who came after him, got pointed toward the open kitchen the very first day.

One of the meanest things I ever heard of in a foster family had to do with food. The foster mom and dad had decided Friday should be family night, a fine idea on the face of it. When the wall calendar showed week's end, they got out the popcorn and everyone gathered around a big, buttery bowl.

Well, not quite everyone. The parents sent the foster kids upstairs, so the only part of the popcorn those youngsters got was the mouth-watering aroma, drifting up from the warmth below. The little party was for "family," you see.

John Masefield wrote,

> He who gives a child a treat
> Makes joy-bells ring in heaven's street.

Is there a special spot in hell reserved for those who hold a treat just out of a child's reach?

Surely only one fair way exists to behave toward a foster child, and that is the same way a parent behaves toward a biological one. Same treats. Same rules.

Many of our foster sons and daughters came to us with little enough reason to respect adults or their authority. Our relatively laid-back style worked most of the time: We minimized rules but insisted on the ones we had.

Our fostering began in the '60s and '70s, a time of social upheaval, of turbulence over civil rights and women's rights. It was the hippie era.

Back then, some folks made a fuss about the length of a young man's hair; they tended to frown at a lad who chose that look. This concerned us, but we took our stand on other issues: We needed to have everybody in school—no exceptions unless you were unconscious. We needed to know everybody's whereabouts—no exceptions unless you were abducted. We needed to see everybody home by curfew—no exceptions unless you were blown away by a tornado.

We needed nobody doing drugs.

We were realistic enough to understand that some of them would try marijuana, just as we had tried cigarettes at their age. Still, we hoped they wouldn't do it.

We underlined this: If any of them brought drugs into the house, the county could hardly be faulted for yanking away our license as a suitable home for foster children.

Jack and I made a point of never actually asking a social worker or probation officer if loss of our license would be all that likely. The gloomy prospect of the foster kids being snatched away made a powerful anti-drug argument to them and we let it go at that.

So far as we know, only one young person ever actually brought pot under our roof. A couple of the others did not exactly tell on him; they just encouraged us to pose some questions.

It's easy to find something out when you already know it.

Other troubling events may well have been going on that we old fogies will never hear about, and that may be just as well. As the kids confided in one another, they sorted out which things we absolutely had to know, and which things they could spare us. They figured out who could safely stay quiet, and who should be persuaded to 'fess up.

Our probation officer warned us that we would go through a honeymoon period with each of our foster kids, a tense time for them in a new setting when they would be trying hard to fit in.

This would almost always be followed by a time of testing.

They had to know what would happen if they blew it. Sometimes foster placements don't work out. Would we send them away? Some kids elect to find that out sooner rather than later, before they get too attached.

Did we really mean they had to be home on time? Did we really mean they had to go to every class? Typically, they would push the rules both at home and at school to check out the consequences.

One of our boys was suspended three times in his first three weeks with us for smoking and skipping classes. He got in-school suspension: Every free moment of his day and for an hour after school, he sat in a study hall where quiet was enforced. When he got home, we grounded him. That meant restriction to the house, no inviting friends over and no phoning friends.

What a bore. He quit smoking in school and he quit skipping classes.

Our wise probation officer taught us not to be caught up in misguided sympathy for our foster kids. He said, "If kids have come from a garbage life, that helps explain what they might do, but should never excuse it." He stressed the need for consistency and logical consequences when kids stray off course.

So that's what we tried for.

One night when I thought the whole crew had trooped off to a movie together, I found Roger sitting in the kitchen by himself.

"Roger! How come you didn't go to the movie with all the other kids?"

He looked at me quizzically.

"Don't you remember, Mom? You grounded me!"

Sometimes so much was going on that we couldn't call to mind who was under house arrest and who wasn't. Ah, well. They kept it straight even when we couldn't.

Our relaxed style did not suit every teen who came to us. Some needed more structure.

Like Warren.

Warren only stayed with us for two weeks. He was a social-worker placement who knew not a one of us when he came. We had little chance to connect.

One Saturday afternoon we took all the kids to the Minneapolis Institute of Arts. I forget what special exhibit was on that some of them wanted to see. We wandered off in our several separate ways in that great, whopping, inspiring space, according to inclination. Whichever kids took Warren under their wings reported that when they turned around, he was nowhere to be found.

It's not so much that the Art Institute wasn't his kind of place; we weren't his kind of folks. He seized his first chance to split.

We've always thought it was pretty classy of Warren, to disappear there among the masterpieces.

We were greatly relieved when his social worker tracked him down safely a day or two later. She placed him in a group home, where they keep better tabs on their kids. We were a kind of group home ourselves, I suppose, but the one he ended up in had professionals for house parents.

We had two other short-term lodgers.

I think of Karla as morning mist. She settled in briefly and pleasantly, graduated from high school a few months later, drifted away and was gone. The school counselor only said that Karla needed us for a short time. She never mentioned why. Was there anything in Karla's history that might affect her behavior? No. That's all we had to know.

Sometimes more specifics unfolded as we lived together with our teens and they came to trust us. But that was always their decision.

Bill, like Karla near graduation, was memorable chiefly for his empty pie pans. Apparently he would buy a pie, eat the whole thing himself and then stash the tin under his bed, where we discovered an impressive collection after his departure.

Which brings up the topic of cleaning the house. Jack and I were both working full-time, he as journalist, I as teacher. With such an active, sizable brood, we obviously needed the kids' help to keep the Board of Health at bay.

So every Friday night we made a list of the most urgent jobs and posted it on the refrigerator door, the refrigerator being the one place every kid was sure to go. When Saturday morning came, the first ones up could choose the cushy jobs, while the slug-a-beds were left to clean the bathrooms. By the time it all got done sometime on Saturday, the house looked reasonably habitable.

As for the rest of the week, averting our eyes was always an option.

3.
Mishaps and Misadventures

THE DAY OF THE Mysterious Sleeping Stranger began like any other.

Joan, the youngest of the original three, was the current occupant of the coveted bedroom at the far end of the lower level. Early that morning, I went down to give her a gentle prod. Our family count stood at just Joan and one foster teen at that time; no one was sleeping in the beds that had partially taken over the rec room outside our daughter's door.

Only somebody was. Sleeping down there. Somebody I had never seen before.

I crept past him.

"Wake up, sweetie," I said to Joan. "Who on Earth is that man out there?"

"What man?" she asked, coming out of her fog.

"Well," said I to this daughter in the buff, "you'd better slip your robe on and come look."

We tiptoed out of her room and peered down at the interloper, still snoozing peacefully.

"I've never seen him before," Joan whispered.

Figuring that he must enjoy some connection to the family, we went about our morning business. After a time, up the stairs the stranger clumped to join us in the kitchen.

I had been considering various greetings. I offered, "Good morning. Would you like some breakfast?"

"Oh, no thank you," he replied with sleepy courtesy. "I'm on my way to meet your son. He gave me your keys last night because I didn't have a place to stay."

I had a word with the son later in the day.

"But, Mother," he protested, "that was Jeff. You remember Jeff."

He forgot that time had transformed the callow stripling we used to know into a well-muscled, richly bearded young man.

Jack the Younger made rather a habit of giving out family keys and forgetting to mention the fact. Some time later, he and Nancy were both living in New York; while her apartment was small, his was tiny. Enter another of Jack's friends, just back from overseas, weary from a long flight, homeless for the night.

Nancy returned from work, opened her door, stepped over the threshold and stopped cold. A total stranger was conked out on her bed.

She took off her shoes and pitched them at him.

"Tell me who you are and what you're doing here, or I'll scream for the police," she said.

Sensible young woman, that Nancy. Kindly, too: She still speaks to her brother.

Jack the Younger hardly meant to cause a rumpus. Neither did Roger, on The Day of the Wreck of the Lower Level.

I was upstairs that afternoon, peeling potatoes. Any number of young people were down below, clattering around, bouncing from game to game.

Then it got very, very quiet.

That makes moms very, very nervous.

"What's happening down there?" I called out.

"Don't come down, Mom. You don't need to come down. Everything's going to be fine."

"Going to be" was the part I didn't like.

At this point, call to mind a pruning bomb. Pruning bombs are pressurized cans of black, tarry gunk for spraying on a tree after lopping off a big limb; the gunk seals the wound.

Roger had set up a dart board on the shelf where a pruning bomb was stashed.

Roger's aim that day proved less true than William Tell's.

When the dart punctured the bomb, it let go its contents with an enthusiasm normally seen at grand finales on the Fourth of July. It sprayed its sticky goo in a spectacular arc. It made speckled kids. Speckled walls. A speckled dresser. And speckled clothes that lay in a box, waiting for my mending hand.

There the loyal siblings were, wiping away at the mess and mostly making it worse, trying to help their flabbergasted brother clean it up before parental wrath came down upon him.

Dismay, yes. Wrath, no. Did he do it deliberately? Naah.

Lemon walls can be repainted and maple dressers restored.

We never did get around to the dresser. It's going to stay the way it is. I've developed rather an affection for its spotted face.

As for the box of raggedy clothes, I pitched it out without a pang. Another carton of buttonless shirts, drooping hems and damaged seams soon took its place, a silent nag on a basement shelf. So where is Roger when I need him?

That whole episode had scared Roger, new enough with us to be unsure of his foster mom's reaction. He was also embarrassed.

Teenagers, poor dears, tend not only to embarrass themselves. They also live in terror of what mortifying thing their parents might do or say in front of their friends.

In my own self-conscious adolescence, I was silly enough to find myself squirming when in the company of my own Mum, a woman wise enough to know when the opinions of others simply shouldn't matter.

Note that my mother never in her life weighed so much as 100 pounds, and that she peaked at just under 5 feet tall. She was the epitome of "petite."

Now consider the fact that my family would occasionally go out to a restaurant for dinner.

"I don't like to eat with my chin on the table," Mum would say. So we would go into the restaurant and she would ask for a baby's high chair. And she would sit in it.

Never mind that what she did made perfect sense. Had a school friend happened by to see her perched there, I would have disappeared like the Cheshire cat. It would have been no toothy grin I left behind. It would have been a whole scarlet face.

Turn now to when I became the parent.

I have always liked to sing. I warble everywhere, including when cruising the aisles of a store. I am hardly conscious of it and I am barely audible. But if the young folks living with us wanted to shop and were too young to drive, they suffered the ill luck of finding themselves at the mall with their mother.

They would drop several paces behind. Embarrassed, you know.

So who richly deserved the red face on the Day of the Pet Shop Scandal? I did, that's who.

It happened in a Christmas season when we had a full house, with Jack the Elder and me seriously outnumbered by seven teens at their rambunctious best. With a shared need to go gift-shopping, the kids and I piled into the family station wagon.

We split at the mall, making a pact on when to meet. The "where" was easy: at the pet store, which would provide entertainment for early arrivers. Besides, I needed kitty litter and this particular place carried it in frugal 50-pound bags.

Nancy, our first-born, had just come home from her first term at college, old enough at last actually to want to be with her mom.

Shopping accomplished, she and I arrived first at the rendezvous.

I suppose it was the playful kittens that reminded her.

"Mom, did you know that catnip is a form of marijuana? That's why cats go cuckoo when you give it to them—they're stoned."

I said I hoped this was not all she was going to learn her freshman year.

I remember that I was only half attending. My mind was taken up with grocery lists, dinner plans and roll call as my young bloods rambled in.

At that moment, a clerk appeared. Ah, yes, my kitty-litter errand.

"May I help you?" he asked.

I blurted out, "Yes, please. I'd like 50 pounds of marijuana."

The clerk looked taken aback. The young bloods exploded.

Making a recovery a good deal quicker than my own, the clerk said, "Sure, I could do that for you, but not right here."

Which set the young bloods off again, who could hardly wait to get home to tell their father.

It was another Christmas that brought us The Day of the Bloody Kitchen Caper. That was the Christmas of young adults hustling home to Minnesota to join their high school siblings for the holidays—all but David, who had joined the Marines after his high-school graduation and was stationed in California, half a continent away.

It was especially hard for me to think of him that far from us because of a situation some time back, just before Jack and I were married. Our wedding date was set for December 29. My husband-to-be was working in Minneapolis until two days beforehand and I was at home in Maryland, helping with final preparations.

Jack was new at his job. None of his co-workers realized he would be alone on Christmas Day. He was renting quarters from a couple who had gone out-of-town for several days. He was alone in the house.

So what did my fiancé have for his Christmas dinner? Cold pork-and-beans, eaten out of the can.

I could have wept at the news.

All those years later, the Marines would do better than that for David's dinner; I knew that perfectly well. Still, with everybody else heading home, there sat the cold pork-and-beans in the back of my brain.

Well, that was how it was and what could I do? I shook myself off, counted heads and my blessings, and got ready for Christmas again.

Little did I dream that this would bring on the Bloody Kitchen Caper, signaled by the drama of triple-recipe cookie dough deserted in mid-batch.

On that memorable baking day, my husband and I had sallied forth to shop, leaving the cooking to Jack the Younger and his sister Nancy. Hours later, we staggered home under a load of packages that would have done credit to Santa himself. We walked into the kitchen and stopped, staring.

The oven was still on but not a soul was home. We saw cookies, iced. Cookies, bald. Dough, abandoned. Frosting, stiff. And sprinkled over all, bright red dots of cinnamon candy.

Oh, yes. And a note.

The note read, "Don't worry about the mess. We'll clean it up when we get home. We've gone someplace."

Maternal instincts went on Red Alert.

"Something is wrong," I fretted.

"Nonsense. They've gone someplace," their daddy soothed. He is good at keeping me calm.

Soon after, our two eldest came home. They'd gone someplace, all right—to the emergency room. Three stitches dangled over our son's right eye.

What had they been doing? Dancing in the kitchen. How came the head cut? From a close encounter with the hood over the cooktop. Why all the red cinnamon candy? To keep us from worrying, in case they missed some spots as they wiped up the blood before driving off for help. And why the dancing to begin with? Oh, that—because they felt like it.

Only there was another reason that they weren't telling.

Their brother, he of the United States Marine Corps, had called his siblings with the sweet news that he would be with us after all. He pledged the others to secrecy until his arrival in the wee hours. This unexpected furlough was all it took to inspire that cavorting around the kitchen.

Fast forward now to 3 a.m., with my husband and me tucked up in bed. There came a shuffling and a giggling in the hall outside our room. There came an opening of our door and a tip-toeing in of whispering, tittering figures. There came a breathing of soft words into my sleepy ear: "Wake up, Mom. Merry Christmas."

And so it was the Christmas of a head cut and stitches over an eye. The Christmas of red cinnamon candies shielding parents from panic. The Christmas of soft words, sweet news and a family circle, complete.

4.

School on a See-Saw

WE PULLED STRINGS LIKE manic puppeteers to get tutors, appropriate classes and top-notch counselors for our foster kids. Some of them needed advocates as desperately as wilting plants need water, so advocates we were.

In our files smolders a letter about David, forwarded from his former school: "There is not one chance he will complete high school. He has not been in any class more than four or five times."

Then he came our way. Snared between us, an alert school staff and new siblings applying arm twists, he had little hope of getting away with class-skipping. Still, his grades that first quarter were C, D, F and an incomplete. His scholastic see-saw was still way down.

But wait! At the end of the last semester of his senior year, that same young man produced a report card that boasted an A in all four academic subjects. He did it, he said, as a gift to us.

David looked great in his cap and gown.

In another file we have a note from David's brother, Roger.
He left it on the kitchen table for us one afternoon: "Dear mom
I and at Reuben house and if it ok if I seep over."

It was okay if he slept over. It was not okay that he was a
sophomore in high school when he wrote that note. We called
in the tutors.

Roger did not stay with us long enough to graduate, but he
found one teacher—just one—who made him feel something
other than stupid in the nearly three years he lived with us.
Somebody please clone that teacher!

Somewhat later came a foster daughter who once struck us
dumb with dismay in a restaurant.

It happened on a long-anticipated mini-vacation in Chi-
cago. One of my all-time favorite family photos was taken then,
when I turned around in time to snap Tania and the three originals walking arm-in-arm down the street, sporting matching
on-an-outing smiles.

On Friday night we went to a classy place for dinner—we
were splurging, after all. Tall, slender Tania looked terrific; she
always did, no matter what she wore.

On this occasion she had donned her gray wool suit with
the gray satin lapels, and heads turned when she walked in on
the arm of her equally tall, spiffily dressed brother Jack.

When the waitress came around to her, Tania ordered a
hamburger. At another good dining place Saturday night, she
ordered a hamburger again. When she asked for the same on
Sunday noon, Jack the Younger spoke up.

"Tania, why don't you try something different? You can
have anything you want."

She answered in a whisper that thundered in our ears,
"Jackson, I can't read the menu."

She was in 10th grade.

Our son recovered first. "Leave it to me," he said. "I will
order for you and it will be the best meal you ever ate."

Humiliation fell away and she felt like a queen.

She was a queen who still could not read a menu. But with the help she needed, that same young girl bounded ahead three years in reading comprehension in two triumphant semesters.

Up sprang her see-saw.

Tania looked great in her cap and gown.

What happened to those three youngsters to help them shake off the shackles of near-illiteracy? Teachers happened.

David was a tough, street-wise black kid from the inner city when he hit the halls of our virtually all-white suburban high school. He came close to calamity on one of his first days. He saw a babe in the hall, petite, blond and beautiful. Never one to pass up an opportunity, he backed this vision up against a wall and turned on the charm.

A potential disaster was defused with the timely arrival of David's friend and foster brother, Jack the Younger. He took one horrified look.

"David, back off! That's a teacher!" he said.

To her everlasting credit and our everlasting gratitude, Bonnie Nelson, the teacher-babe, elected not to bounce our boy into the principal's office or anywhere else except back to class.

Clearly this was no ordinary kid, so he was placed in an extraordinary setting: a school-within-a-school for students who needed teachers with special skills.

Harsh teachers to make young hooligans knuckle under? Hardly.

Upbeat teachers who expected every kid to do well? Exactly.

What may have mattered most was this: They cared and they showed it.

They were teachers like Elsie Evans, who sent David a Christmas card featuring a black man and his son. David opened it and said, "That's me and my dad."

Teachers like David Cade, who wrote a note to us and another to our own David at the end of his junior year. The message to us praised "the enthusiasm and interest with which

David completed all assigned material." This, about the formerly dedicated class-skipper, whose own note from his teacher read, "I'm looking forward to seeing you in the fall. Call me this summer if you get time."

Teachers like Marilyn Hoisve, in whose classroom Tania was lucky enough to land. Her letter home about Tania read, "She is willing to try any assignment I give her. Her progress is so exciting!"

It's not only grade-school parents who post notes on refrigerator doors.

And then there was Ert Hermerding, a speech teacher in junior high school.

We first heard his name when I asked Roger, at that time a fairly new arrival in our home, how school was going. I asked with breath held, knowing how hard learning was for this lad, so far behind.

He hesitated. Then, "I like Mr. Hermerding's class. I don't feel dumb in there."

Like Mahatma Gandhi, Hermerding tried to make every person feel secure in his presence. He had arranged for Roger to take tests orally; reading skills far below par seemed a poor reason for a speech-class grade to suffer. It was the only course in which Roger did well.

That's one of the teachers we want cloned.

The day Roger brought our dog to school was his finest moment in that class, and also his most perilous. Our Shetland sheepdog was to be a lively prop for Roger's demonstration speech. The lad had practiced at home, but he grew so nervous in front of the class that he absently wound the long training leash around his own neck. Our sheltie, still attached to the business end, luckily gave no sudden lurches, so injury was averted and the speech was a success.

Some of our foster kids did exceptionally well academically, despite the issues that dogged them from their earlier lives.

Cathy was my student before she was our foster kid. In my quarter-century of teaching, she and Steve Brandt were the two best writers of high-school age whom it was my good fortune to have in class—this, followed by the further good luck of having them both come to live in our home.

Cathy moved through her world in near-silence in those days. It was through her extraordinary writing that she could release her feelings.

She was enrolled in a creative writing class taught by my colleague, Al Shaff. When summer came, he brought her to a workshop intended for adults, where she was not only by far the youngest, but also the best fiction writer.

The workshop instructor said he could not find any way of doing a detailed critique of her stories. "Your imaginative and expressive gifts are of such a high order, that I would be reluctant to question anything in them. I have made a few marks, but only as suggestions...These pieces are obviously disturbing to me, as they should be. I won't forget them, and I feel privileged to have read them."

Cathy said little when she came home. In those days, saying little was what she did. What did that matter? She could write. And she showed me the non-critique. What more did I need to know?

Her creativity pulled in the whole family the next summer when she earned an English credit by writing, directing and acting in a film called "Midnight Biter." All of us in the family had roles in this high drama; it featured a number of suicides, all committed by simulated leaps off our back deck.

Jack the Younger was a vampire and Jack the Elder, a plumber. One of Cathy's sisters played a mad woman and another, a seductress. There was a revolutionary. There was a gypsy fortune-teller. I, a dedicated non-smoker, was required by my role to dangle a cigarette. Even various ones of our youngsters' current boyfriends had bit parts.

Seldom has such a motley collection of characters come together in a single story.

Baby Alan, then about a year old, played a key role. First he solved the film's riddle by licking frosting off a cake (you had to be there). Ultimately, he crawled up a slope with "The End" written on his diaper.

Cathy earned the English credit.

Like Cathy and Steve, Daniel was smart, so smart that his test scores soared off the charts. Emancipated from his parents while living with us, he commanded few resources for college expenses.

That's when our friend Gary Joselyn kicked in, a professor with multiple contacts at the University of Minnesota. He helped put together a package of scholarships, grants, loans and work-study jobs that would pay for Daniel's whole freshman year.

Daniel did not make it past the first semester. "Three of my four professors are dumber than I am," he exclaimed, quitting in disgust.

Well, of course! Almost everybody was dumber than Daniel. Alas, he did not have the patience to jump through educational hoops.

When he died accidentally a few years later, he had made a good life for himself as a store manager and volunteer fireman. No longer did his elders pull long faces and point out that he was failing to live up to his potential, as they had for most of his young life. Never mind that he might have been another Stephen Hawking; he found contentment.

And so must we.

Our family litany of exceptional teachers includes a few who were exceptionally bad. Let us dwell with distaste on only one, the junior high school teacher who upset us most.

It started in our kitchen one night when the teenagers on dish duty began flicking wet towels at one another, as teenagers will. For once, Roger the scamp was getting the best of his older brothers, until one of them made a show of taking off his belt.

Roger turned ashen, made a strangled sound and ran from the room. What could we conclude? Before he came into our lives, someone used a belt to beat him.

Soon after that, Roger sought me out. Big-eyed, subdued, casting about for words, he finally asked, "Mom, did you know that my gym teacher paddles the last one out of the pool?"

I mulled that over for a moment and then asked my own careful question: "Were you the last one out of the pool today?"

Next morning I called the teacher. I applauded the school district policy against corporal punishment. That being the case, paddling was clearly inappropriate, no matter how light or symbolic the smacks.

I thought my reasonable point had been reasonably received. But Roger's style was always more steady than swift and the swats came again.

This time I made an appointment with the principal, marched off to school and grew more explicit. If our boy was causing problems, let us know; we will do our part at home to encourage better behavior.

But for this youngster, any physical punishment was traumatic. Discipline, yes. Paddling, no. Not for any student. Especially not for this student.

I thought I was pretty plain about it.

The swats kept coming.

It takes a lot to get my dander up.

That did it.

I fired off a white-hot letter to the principal that was still steaming when I slipped it in the mail slot. So help me, I said, this new son of mine was not going to get knocked around any more. Paddling, I said, was just a new twist on the cuffing he'd been getting all his life. "Stop," I said.

This is how I ended the letter: "Under no circumstances is any person in the school ever to lay a hand on him again. Unless, of course, you want to hug him."

The swatting stopped. I don't know about the hugging, except at home.

5.
Little Brother

A TINY PIECE OF glass fell out of Roger's forehead and tinkled onto his dinner plate one night. We must have missed it when we were plucking little bits of the storm door out of that forehead earlier in the day. Luckily, he got to laughing at the table and that dislodged the final fragment.

It was a minor mishap, nothing compared to what happened later.

When he first came skipping into our house, Roger was about 12, a lovable youngster, small for his age, the very model of an impish kid. He quickly assumed the little-brother role in the family.

For instance, he would taunt the older boys, first taking care to be poised for prudent flight. On the afternoon in question, he had propped the main door open, only to have the storm door fail to give beneath his hand. Hence the fragments.

Of course there was teasing in the house and some teenage rough-and-tumble. But on the whole, the young people did much to help each other.

Joan, our youngest daughter, has always been shy of public speaking. Whenever she had to do it, she remembers that "Roger would graciously sit and listen to me give a talk, becoming my practice audience of one." Joan, for her part, helped Roger with his homework.

Roger was fun. He skipped when he walked. He was a tease with a tender heart, quick to give affection and hungering for it himself. Such heart and such hunger prompted this note to his foster dad, just as he wrote it:

> Dad them no better time them now to say I am glad
> to be with you.
> love one
> love two
> love all of us
> Happy Father Day many retuns love Roger

The prized, faintly grubby paper is ragged on the edge where he tore it from his notebook. Who needs pricey cards? Poets do not plead with eloquence more simple nor a spirit more generous.

He spent three Father's Days as one of our own. Then tensions eased in his biological family, giving Roger and his brother David a weighty choice. David was nearer to high school graduation and elected to stay with us. Roger packed up his precious jeans—only once did we ever see him in a suit—and returned to his birth home.

Helping to reunite families is what foster parents are supposed to do. Nobody told us it would be so hard.

Roger was in 10th grade at the time. Within three weeks, he had dropped out of school. A charitable estimate would have put his reading at the 8th grade level.

He went on with his life and we with ours. In the years that followed, we stayed in touch as best we could.

Some time later, long enough so Roger was a grown man, I stumbled upon a literacy center geared to helping adults with his hidden handicap—the inability to read, write or compute with the ease most of us take for granted. Why hadn't I thought of that before? Roger and I walked in together to check it out and meet the director.

Roger posed a question: "Is this like a class with one teacher and lots of kids?"

The director sensed the wounds that lay behind the words. Year after dreary year, Roger had been lost in a swarm of youngsters who caught on quicker than he did. Too many students share his lot: They get sick and fall behind, or their folks make little of school, or nobody notices a learning disability, or.....

So they drag from class to class feeling stupid, collecting veiled bruises but precious little from books.

The director got the message.

"Come look," she said.

We saw half a dozen adults pecking away at terminals in a computer room. We saw a watchful tutor spring into action when a learner lamented, "I've done this dumb thing three times and I still don't get it."

We saw one person, struggling with multiplication, get a tactful "I bet you can do better" on his computer screen at the end of an exercise. Another, having more success with fractions, earned, "Excellent work! Thanks for playing."

We saw one woman with smile wrinkles and salt-and-pepper hair studying how to tell time. She stared at the clock on her screen for three minutes, maybe four. Then, "10:33!" she announced to the room at large. No laurel-crowned champion ever glowed with grander satisfaction.

Roger saw. He stayed.

I phoned him on the evening of his second scheduled visit.

"How'd it go, dear?" I asked. He could not have known how hard I was clutching the phone.

"I was there two hours," he reported. "I have a headache, but I'm going back on Thursday."

Then, as always, he asked about me. When was I going to write that book about our adventures as a foster family, the one I had been mulling over so long?

"C'mon, Mom," he urged. "It will give me some reading material. They'll like that at the literacy center."

Not bad for a person who had dodged books all his days.

Sometimes Roger wasn't so good at dodging.

A few months after he moved back with his birth family, he called me from an emergency room.

His words came strained and strung together: "Hi Mom I'm hurt I'm in the hospital I've gotta have surgery but you don't have to come and see me."

Someone had hit him in the face with a vacuum cleaner. Not the hose from the vacuum cleaner. The vacuum cleaner.

I got to him in 20 minutes. What he had really been saying was, "How SOON are you not going to come and see me?" We all need a mom when we've been smacked in the mouth.

His jaw got wired together and he mended well.

But the next time somebody took him to a hospital, he was dead before he got there.

Roger was in his early 30s when he died. He was killed in a stupid argument in a Minneapolis apartment, shot in the chest, his sudden, brutal death denying those who cared about him the blessed chance to say good-bye.

And it wasn't even his argument. A friend had said, "Somebody owes me money. Come help me collect." Was it desperately bad luck? Or did his friend maneuver Roger first through the door?

Roger was the second of our foster sons to die.

Daniel had made it through rough waters, settling comfortably at last into a job and a marriage, when he was fatally injured. One malignant summer evening, he was hit in the head by a batted ball, a pure accident, a freakish, improbable thing, a tragedy that none could foresee and nothing could prevent.

Roger's death was all too predictable. For young black males, the leading cause of death is homicide. That horror has a face to it now. His face.

My husband and I sometimes wondered if it made sense to bring black kids into a nearly all-white suburb and a nearly all-white school. We knew enough to know that we knew nothing about what it meant to be black.

That wasn't giving our black children enough credit. They all worked out their own ways of dealing with racial taunts.

David was tougher and way more street-wise than any swaggering suburban punk who dared to call him "nigger." He just knocked the punk down. Roger stood tall—a good trick when you're a shrimpy kid—and made light of the insults; he was a better man than those who hurled them. Our daughter Tania scrunched herself down in the corner of a new classroom until she felt safe. Her teachers reported that it was never long before she uncorked her usual bubbly self.

By lucky chance, a letter to the editor from an officer of the National Association for the Advancement of Colored People (NAACP) appeared on the pages of our local newspaper scant days after Roger's death. The writer called it "balderdash" to think white families can't provide what black children need.

He wrote, "All children are better off in a loving, secure home environment. That should be our main concern in determining the 'appropriate' placement of African-American children, not the color of the family."

To a pair of grieving foster parents, the letter brought much comfort.

As child and man, Roger made some of his own trouble; don't we all? And yet there was an innocence about him that trouble never touched.

He came among strangers when hardly more than a child, to live in their home and by their rules, and he tried very, very hard to please them. Lots of folks in this world are better dressers and better lookers than Roger was; lots of them are brainier. But I never met a one who was sweeter.

He came to those strangers—to us—because he wanted to be with his brother, who loved him. Ultimately, he was buried in his brother's suit.

But we too came to love Roger, and he came to know it.

There was that. At least there was that.

6.

Not with the Nigger-Lover

ROGER WAS SMALLER, MILDER and more vulnerable than his brother David.

Small, mild and vulnerable does not equate to lack of moral fiber.

Take, for instance, an encounter at a small, secluded beach favored by teens where Joan and Laura often swam. Once when they turned up with Roger, a lazy, sunny afternoon turned suddenly ugly.

What was a nigger boy doing there with a couple of white chicks?

The chicks were ready to draw red blood on Roger's behalf. He remained unruffled.

"It doesn't matter what they call me," he told his incensed sisters. "I know who I am."

Not bad for a high school sophomore.

Adults occasionally show themselves to be as blatantly prejudiced as those white boys on the beach.

Soon after David came to live with us, it occurred to Jack the Elder that there might be a knack to cutting a black person's hair, so he checked it out with his customary barber. Could he do a good job for our foster son?

"It's not that I can't," the barber said. "It's that I won't. If you bring him in and I cut his hair, he'll wish I hadn't."

Jack found a new barber.

Another adult of our acquaintance equaled that barber's bias. He was the father of our son's friend Daniel.

By the time Daniel was a junior in high school, he and his dad teetered at the breaking point. The lad hung out at our house a lot; we found him clever and witty. But he was also a hot-blooded liberal who never in his life held an opinion without bringing it to public notice.

This jalapeno pepper of a kid came up against his exceptionally conservative parent one time too many. He passed on to us his father's parting volley: "If you don't like it here, get out and go find yourself someplace else. You can live anywhere you want, except with your long-haired, hippie, nigger-loving friend."

That would be our son Jack.

But moving into our house with Jack was exactly what Daniel wanted to do. After many weeks and by a tortuous route, that is what he eventually was able to do.

Since Daniel was living with us unofficially, our attorney fretted about the possible consequences if something unexpected happened. Suppose Daniel fell off the roof or down a hole? His parents ultimately agreed to sign a letter consenting to his housing arrangement, which happily proceeded void of bizarre accidents.

Free-spirited Daniel never bumped up against our school district's dress code. Rather, it was David who did that, scant days after he came to live with us. Since he arrived with only the clothes he had on, I took him shopping almost as soon as he came in the door. The younger set knew of the dress-code details, and I suppose I did too, but I had forgotten them.

On the school-day in question, I remember thinking how nice his new white T-shirt looked against his warm brown skin.

I was teaching at a school 20 miles away when a phone call summoned me to come and pick up our new arrival: He needed to go home and get a proper shirt, I was told, because he was wearing underwear to class. I made a mad dash over and back on my lunch break, grumbling inwardly.

Unmindful of the dress code, the parental unit in our house (Jack the Elder and I) had never taken a stand on whether a T-shirt was, or was not, underwear.

Not so Jack the Younger.

His social studies class had lately discussed the civil rights struggle, including the policy of non-violent protest. He had duly noted the tactic of taking a stand on a deeply held conviction and then bearing the consequences without complaint.

He decided to take on the dress code. He wore a white T-shirt to school.

Twice teachers passing him in the hall called out, "Goodwin, don't you know you are supposed to wear a shirt over that?"

"Yes, sir, I know."

All day, that's how the consequences went.

There were none.

No one pulled him aside, took him to the office, called his mom and sent him home to change. The distasteful, unintended message: How you are treated in this world may depend on who you are.

Sometimes their own experience at the hands of bigots confused our foster kids about the appropriate reaction to outside events. When I came home one day, David was waiting for me. Quite without expression, he gave me the news that Alabama's George Wallace had been shot. The black teen well knew this man was the governor who had vowed to maintain segregation by standing in the schoolhouse door.

How severely flawed the man's stance. How sorely tempting to rejoice at his misfortune.

David's basic decency kept him from it. But if not that, what should he feel? As we talked, he found within himself the capacity to hate the sin but not the sinner.

Other times, circumstances came across as so incredibly cruel that our kids had no difficulty figuring out where they should stand. One night Tania and I were watching an episode of Alex Haley's "Roots." She was appalled at the brutal behavior of some slave-holders in the pre-Civil War south. In a cry wrung from her heart, she exclaimed, "Mom, they shouldn't treat a dog that way."

Slavery no longer exists in America. Prejudice does.

You need not be black to suffer its sting. You could be on welfare. You should not have to endure dim-witted slurs because of your circumstances.

Perhaps you are on welfare because you are jobless, injured, elderly or ill.

Or perhaps you are like my friend Nan, who was sitting in a rocking chair nursing her third baby when her husband told her he was leaving her for another woman. She picked herself up, shook the dust of him off her feet and went back to college—which she had left after her second year to support her husband while he finished. With the help of welfare funds and a succession of scholarships, she made her way through college and then law school.

Now she is a public defender. In much of her work, she helps others to struggle upright again.

Or perhaps you are like my Cambodian friends, who made a perilous flight through the jungle with their children, evading soldiers, sleeping in trees, finally reaching America after a period in a refugee camp in Thailand.

When I first met them, they lived in public housing in St. Paul. The parents slept in the living room. The four children slept in double bunk beds crammed into the second bedroom. Barely enough room remained to walk between the bunks.

The largest bedroom was reserved for a study for the children, with wall-to-wall desks and an unabridged dictionary. There were no curtains on the windows but the children had that dictionary.

The parents, highly educated in their native country, spoke only limited English. They worked at entry-level jobs, investing all the time and energy they had into the education of their children.

Today, every one of those children has earned a master's degree. All have become naturalized citizens, the new blood with which America renews itself.

Or perhaps you are on welfare because you are a child—a foster child.

I drove our son Daniel to see a doctor once, not my personal physician but his own. I had never been in that waiting room and I could not help noticing a sign on the wall: "Welfare clients should show there (sic) card's (sic) at every visit."

The longer I waited for Daniel, the more those errors troubled me. Finally I went up to the desk and, as tactfully as I could, I told the receptionist what I thought she would want to know.

Her response was, "That's all right. Welfare clients wouldn't know the difference anyway."

Fixing her with a fierce look, I snapped, "The only thing worse than your grammar is your humanity."

Normally, I am pretty mild-mannered, but boy, did that feel good.

Being on welfare is a temporary condition; it sometimes brings insult, but seldom injury. Consider the different situation for those who are gay.

Some gay people proudly wear pink triangles like those pinned to homosexuals in Nazi Germany, knowing that they may face prejudice that is irrational, even vicious. Only consider the ferocious murder of young Matthew Shephard to understand the awful truth of that.

The hardest part of coming out of the closet must be, for many, the revelation to one's parents. When she was a grown-up and on her own, our foster daughter Cathy could not go to her birth mother and reveal that the woman with whom she was living was her lover as well as her friend.

It was not merely that she thought her mother might drive her away or disown her; she thought it possible that her mother might not let her out of the house alive. After all, this was the mother who for years had believed her daughter to be demon-possessed.

Still, she needed to share this important part of herself with her foster parents—her symbolic parents, if you will. Us.

Since Jack the Elder and I had already guessed, there was no need for Cathy to make a long story of it. We assured this dear woman, once the abused child and outcast in her own family, that nothing could make us happier than to know she had found someone to love who loved her back.

Edna St. Vincent Millay said it like this:

> ...many a man is making friends with death,
> Even as I speak, for lack of love alone.

That goes for women and children, too.

7.
Capers

THE MOST FUN I ever had fooling my family began one December day during my years as a high school teacher. Frank, a good sport and the jolliest of students, walked into homeroom with an enormous box under his arm.

Naturally, I wondered what was in it.

"My Santa suit," he explained.

Then it came to me. "So what are you doing Friday night?"

It so happens that gathering 'round the family board that evening would be several of our teens and young adults, the three then in residence and three more home for the holidays. It was but a few moments' work to furnish Frank with the necessary facts for easy identification: David and Tania were black, for instance, and Joan had long blond hair.

Frank's timing was exquisite. Just as we finished dinner on the appointed night, the doorbell gave a mighty peal. When Jack the Younger answered the summons, trumpets blared. My student had outdone himself: He had brought with him two elves in costume, a.k.a., a couple of his pals from the high school band.

Bearing a bag of candy canes, Frank circled the table.

"Have you been a good little girl this year, Nancy? Ho! Ho! Ho! I'll just bet you have! And how about you, Jackie? Such a fine little fellow!" This to the lad who towered above him at 6'3".

Thus Santa made the rounds, bestowing treats, ruffling hair, kissing the girls and never once mistaking a name.

Not a person in my family had ever seen him before. The farther he got around the ring of diners, the more mystified they grew and the more hilarious it became.

When at last he reached me, I sprang up, threw my arms around him and exclaimed, "Oh, Santa, I love you!" Then he made his exit.

I let confusion reign for a small, delicious interval. Not one of them suspected the truth.

Finally, I confessed. Then I marveled, "Didn't you figure it out when I jumped up and kissed him?"

"Oh, Mother, that was no help," answered one. "You kiss everybody who comes to this house."

It's not true, of course. I have never once kissed our letter carrier.

A rowdy dinner of a different sort took place when Jack the Elder was away one evening, leaving me to maintain order alone. The father of the family can conjure up a stern face no more readily than I, but at least when the two of us were on parental duty together, we were not so seriously outnumbered.

The trouble began innocently enough when one of the teens put together a strawberry shortcake. Rummaging in the refrigerator, he found the classic topping: whipped cream in a can primed to spring out at the touch of a button.

David got first dibs but he "forgot" to aim down at his dessert, thereby splotching his brother Jack, who grabbed the can and splotched back.

All others, self-respecting teens that they were, demanded their turn.

No contemporary artist flinging paint on canvas could have outdone that crew. As one or the other snatched the canister, blobs clung to clothes and dripped from faces. Sticky mounds capped hair. A white pox broke out on the tabletop.

Steve, who grew up in an orderly household, was astonished. That is not to say he took no part.

Ah, well. They were good kids. They cleaned it up when the can came up empty.

That was the messiest dinner in memory, although other mealtime havocs have also scored high.

Take the time a grandpa had come from afar to honor a family birthday.

Steve, always a good cook, volunteered to produce the cake.

What a masterpiece he turned out—not so much the cake itself as what crowned it. He had ransacked the cupboards and smothered the frosting with coconut, chocolate chips, miniature marshmallows and jelly beans.

It was a thing to behold, a cake among cakes, the very king of confections.

Until, too near the edge of the kitchen counter, it tipped and dropped.

On the floor.

Just as a kitchen band was about to usher it in.

The cake itself, although now lopsided, held together reasonably well. The same could not be said for the frosting and its adornments. The former masterpiece lay in serious disarray.

Never one to be defeated by so small a setback, Steve picked it all up, shoved the layers back in alignment, gave the smeared toppings an artistic swirl and bore it to the dining room.

Did Grandpa know of the kitchen calamity? He never said a word.

That particular kind of mishap happened only once. When Laura's son reached the toddler stage, mealtime messes of a different sort were a common event.

As he began to feed himself, Alan developed a liking for the feel of food in his hair. He favored pureed green beans, which looked especially revolting.

What he liked even better than food in his hair was food in his ears.

What he liked best of all was food on the floor.

We took to spreading newspapers under and around his high chair. He looked down a lot as he dribbled from his spoon. We thought of it as early literacy training.

When he grew to young manhood, Alan joined the staff of the governor of Minnesota as an intern. Two days later, he was hired as an administrative assistant. I can attest to the fact that his table manners had improved.

Others before Alan did their bit to trash our poor floors.

As a boy, Jack the Younger was helping tidy up after supper. You need to know that the cover of my favorite casserole dish sports a knob too high to allow it to slide easily onto a refrigerator shelf. Simply flipping the lid solves the problem.

This is what I said to Jack the Younger: "Please put the tuna fish with the lid on upside down in the refrigerator."

After pausing to reflect on his mother's strange request, he put the lid on right way up, turned the whole thing over and carefully slid it onto the refrigerator's wire shelf, resting on its wobbly knob.

Then he let go.

The tuna salad hit the floor and splattered in every direction. It was the most comical thing that had ever happened in that kitchen, and his dad and I could not help ourselves. We burst out laughing.

Our son was so offended. As he indignantly pointed out, he had done exactly what I asked him to do.

Of course, he hadn't done it on purpose. Not so with some of his later mischief, deliberately plotted with his siblings.

Nancy's brothers discovered she had a date who would be picking her up at the house one evening. A new acquaintance, he had the misfortune to arrive early at a time when Jack the Elder and I were not home.

The young males in residence—at that time they numbered four—ushered in their unsuspecting prey. They pointed him to a sofa and when he had settled himself, they lined themselves up in facing chairs and began their inquisition.

One can imagine what followed:

"Where are you taking our sister?"

"What will you be doing there?"

"Will anyone she knows be there, too?"

"Who would that be?"

"What time will you bring her home?"

Implied in all this, or possibly stated outright, was the unmistakable message: "Do her wrong and you will find yourself dealing with us."

Nancy appeared, took one appalled look and made her escape with her date. After that night, she never saw him again.

She was the eldest of our brood. As she moved in and out of the house during her college years, she had trouble keeping track of the fluctuating household census.

One summer she was working for the local park board, putting on plays for little kids. One day, the crew of a children's television show arranged to interview the cast. The question they asked of Nancy seemed simple enough: "How many brothers and sisters do you have?"

"Ummm," she said.

"Ahhh," she said.

The total stood at seven that summer. By the time she had counted them up in her head, the camera had moved on.

Sometimes we startled people without intending it. I had made an appointment to give blood and it occurred to me that Daniel had just turned old enough to become a donor. It didn't take much to persuade him and soon we were stretched out on tables side-by-side, arms extended, chatting away while a nurse went back and forth, doing whatever nurses do to look after us.

It was when she realized Daniel was calling me "Ma" that she blurted out, "But he can't be your son! With your blood type and his, that would be impossible!" Then she blanched, thinking she had unwittingly revealed to Daniel some dark family secret about his origins.

David was the startled one on a different day. Fresh from the city and alone at home, he called an emergency number to report a wild animal loose in our yard. The police arrived to find a mild-mannered guinea pig, briefly released by our neighbors to enjoy some free-range grazing.

On another occasion, it was the parents who suffered the scare. Away on a much-needed vacation for two, we were summoned to a telephone with the news that David had been in a fender-bender that mashed the hood of our second auto—the one the kids drove, a Volkswagen the color of buttercups.

Was he all right?

Happily, yes. Whew! The only thing scrambled was the little yellow car itself.

Never before in an accident, David was so worried about the expense that he called us long-distance every day to update us on the insurance report, the estimates and the repairs themselves. We began to think that the phone bill might outdistance the cost of fixing the car.

One other mishap was equally expensive and entirely our fault—Jack the Elder's and mine, that is.

We had bought an outboard motor for our little fishing boat, which we had put in the water at a friend's cabin one weekend. The adults were sitting on shore sipping pre-dinner wine, watching David learn to manage the boat a hundred yards out.

How relaxed we were! How pleasant the tang of the wine, the song of the birds, the scent of the pines, the putt-putt of the shiny new motor!

Until suddenly there was no putt-putt.

Out on the water was David, adrift, peering dumbfounded over the stern.

We had neglected to secure the motor with a chain.

"Drop the anchor!" hollered Jack the Elder, hoping to get a rough reading of the position.

We dove all the next day. We needn't have bothered. The motor rests in peace, buried in the mud on the bottom of that lake.

Our extended family proved unfailingly tolerant of all the goings-on at our address. On one visit, Aunt Margaret and Great-Aunt Jean were bedded down in the only available accommodations at the time: the lower level, laid out dormitory style. A foster son came in late and they never blinked the next morning when they woke up next to a young man to whom they had not been introduced.

The relative adored by all our children, both biological and affectional, was Jack's father, Grandpa Al. He was a gentleman and a scholar, of a kind that is all too rare in any age.

He wrote us once when he was moving that he had just finished packing 40 boxes of books. Said David, astonished, "Has Grandpa read all those books?" Al had long ago made it into the Super Bowl of readers; for that and his many kindly attributes, we knew of no role model we would rather have claimed for our kids.

When he came to see us shortly after Laura moved in with her baby, we related the circumstances of our single mom to this man of a different time. We couldn't help wondering how he would react.

We told how she had given up all thought of college, drastically altering her future plans so she could keep her son and care for him. We told how she had made those decisions thoughtfully, matter-of-factly and without complaint.

Later that day, Grandpa Al said to Laura, "You are the bravest young woman I know."

She wore that like a medal.

Not long after, Laura and 11 others of our children were honored guests at our 25th wedding anniversary, when Jack the

Elder and I renewed our vows.

"Who gives this woman..." said the minister, in the old-fashioned way.

"We do!" they chorused.

Then they announced that they wanted to come on our second-honeymoon trip to Mexico.

"Whoever heard of 12 children on a honeymoon?" we asked.

"Whoever heard of 12 children at a wedding?" they countered.

They didn't get to come, but they threw rice.

It was the last thing we needed.

8.

Crash Landings

I STOOD IN THE office at the school where I was teaching, tears running down my face. My husband had called, wondering—against all probability—if I had used checks randomly and out of sequence, or had not recorded numbers or amounts, he knowing that could hardly be the case, both of us knowing that the only other explanation was that some young person, one of ours, had stolen from us.

And so it was. And so I stood weeping. And so once again we went down that painful path of discovering the "who" and deciding the logical consequences.

For this was not the first time one of our foster teens had been guilty of theft.

Mary and Don Roening, our close neighbors, once suffered a minor house fire involving a cat and a heating pad (the cat survived just fine, thank you). In the confusion that followed, two youngsters who were attached to us stole a coin collection from them and used it in the pop machine at a nearby bowling alley.

Luckily, the owner noticed. He knew the kids. He knew us. Some of the coins, at least, were retrieved and the neighbors, Lord bless them, remained friends.

Karen Bowen, another friend with a cabin and an abundant bunkhouse, invited our whole crew to join her for a lakeshore weekend. At that time we numbered six teens and their parents (us).

It was a deeply troubled friend who came to me a day into the visit to report $10 missing from her purse. We called the kids together for an emergency conference. They suggested that they chip in to make up the amount, a proposal that we rejected.

We said, "Somebody took it. Somebody put it back."

Somebody did. We never knew who. We let the kids figure it out and do the persuading. Although confession is good for the soul, it's all we could think of to do.

We never imagined escaping without crashes when living with all those teens, but we felt wretched whenever some of the debris splattered someone we knew. Count us lucky; we never lost a friend, the coin-collectors and the cabin-owner included.

Many of the kids who came to us had only limited access to childhood's small treasures. Our probation officer confided that one of them had stolen a box of crayons when he was 5 years old. The little boy had never had a crayon of his own and it was unlikely he would ever have found one in his home.

His act of stealing was wrong, of course. But after early and persistent deprivation, it is little wonder that a smattering of our foster teens were sometimes unable to postpone gratification, as unable as a cat presented with a dish of caviar, let alone cream.

On one occasion, one of our boys spent his allowance to buy a road race set we had promised him for Christmas. His mother's birthday came soon after his I-have-to-have-it-now purchase. Predictably, he asked us for money to buy her a present.

He scrubbed and waxed our floors, whether they needed it or not. Only then was he able to buy the gift. Away he went to offer it, wearing brown-and-white striped pants, his brother's borrowed jersey and his spanking new straw hat. The sight of him must have been as much a gift as what he carried in his hands.

Of course, not all of our teens' troubles had to do with money.

To their credit, some of them tried to help with problems back in their birth homes. When one of David's sisters stole checks to buy clothes, his first instinct was to leave us, quit school, go home and find ways for her to sidestep the consequences. It was his brother Jack who persuaded him that the best thing he could do for her was to help her face up to it—and then stay where he was. That was what his absent but well-loved birth father would want.

On one night that had us worried, David, Jack and their friend Mike had a falling out at Mike's house. With everybody mad, David took off on his own.

The two white lads drove straight home and summoned Jack the Elder to help with the search. David was somewhere out there, overwrought, late at night, in a neighboring suburb whose police were not overly friendly to minorities.

He did what we had hoped: He came home to us. Soon after, so did the searchers. The three boys disappeared into Jack's bedroom and came out clear-eyed and squabble-free, with one crash landing averted.

One potential young friend never did join our troop of teens.

We had long looked forward to hosting a foreign student for a year, just as many of our friends had done. However, our application was turned down because the sponsoring organization ruled out placing a high school student in a family where anyone was on probation.

Roger, sweet Roger, had stolen a car in his desperate, successful move to get a judge to place him with us and his brother David. Thereby a student from somewhere overseas missed a chance to become part of an integrated American family. Understandable, we thought, but regrettable.

So there remains the account of one young person who left us with no regrets on either side. Stanley was a high school student whose parents were moving out of the state early in his senior year. A new school at that point in a teen's life usually makes for one unhappy teen, and so it was arranged that he would stay with us.

Little did we suspect what an unpleasant turn that would take.

Stanley's intention was to skip school as often as he could get away with it to spend the day with his girlfriend. He left home at the proper time. He came home at the proper time. He went to some classes but not others. Some days he never showed up in school at all.

At home, he rarely did his share of chores. Not only did he shirk them, he turned sullen when reminded.

Many evenings, he and his girl would go to bars, where Stanley—a husky specimen who looked more in his twenties then his teens—would pull a long face and lie about his "painful experiences in Viet Nam." He told us with some pride that this often cadged him free drinks.

We were appalled. He didn't like it when we said so.

The school sent us absentee notices. We were in touch with his parents. We gave him another chance. He used it to go on doing what he had been doing, which included very, very little in school.

His third quarter report card came limping in the mail with one B, one C, two Ds and two Fs. Little hope remained that he would graduate. He could not live with us if he only pretended to try. By mutual agreement, his parents came to retrieve him and we parted company.

That was the rare crash from which we saw no recovery in the time we had together.

Other kids stumbled too, but we watched with satisfaction as they picked themselves up, changed behavior, built trust with us anew and found the good within themselves.

Some had learned to survive by theft, lies and manipulation. After a while, they didn't do that any more.

One showed us in a single moment how much of a man he had become. That was David. David, so impulsive when we first knew him, reacted to his brother Roger's murder with a maturity that left us awestruck.

Roger died on Thanksgiving Day. David had planned to spend it with his family, but when he arrived, he found the door wide open and no one home. As he stood wondering, his sister and a cousin drove up.

"Your brother has been shot," his cousin said. He could not bring himself to add, "dead."

Neither did he mention a name. David had more than one brother: an older one who had been in various scrapes, and Roger, the younger one who had followed him to us.

David dashed to the hospital. "Where is my brother? He's been shot."

He was brought to a small conference room. A doctor came in.

"I'm so sorry. I could not save your brother Roger."

Roger? Roger?

David crumpled to the floor.

Then he stumbled from the hospital and set out to find the killer.

Several enraged members of Roger's family had already spilled out into the streets. Without a doubt, they knew the man to look for; witnesses had seen the shooting.

David found him first. He summoned the police. At the end of the call he cautioned, "If you are not here in 10 minutes, there won't be anything left for you to question." The police got there in 3.

Thus the man who had done the murder was saved from a swarm of incensed relatives. He was under arrest before the night was out. And was tried. And convicted.

Because David had summoned the police.

9.
Delicate Ground

CATHY HAD A FANTASY that her mother would hold her and let her cry. That, from Cathy, so sorely wounded, was all the proof we needed of the power of the blood tie.

Foster placement is meant to be temporary, unless home situations are so horrendous that children must be taken away for good—for their good and forever. Granted, ours were already in their teens and tended to stay with us until they graduated from high school. Still, getting kids back with their moms and dads has always been a primary goal of foster care.

That meant we needed to tiptoe around whatever history we knew. It meant we needed to connect with those moms and dads in the most constructive ways we could.

We tried to imagine what it must be like for them. Imagined ourselves, judged unfit. Imagined our children taken out our door into an unknown, whether or not they wanted that or even understood it. Imagined an unhappy teen simply preferring to live with some other set of parents.

That made it easier to attempt connections.

It did nothing to make the contacts less awkward. That was especially true of the initial communication after a youngster's arrival.

The fact that Laura took baby Alan out into a storm and carried him through the blowing snow from her house to ours, short though the distance was, made it obvious that a different sort of storm had been raging within the walls four blocks away.

But no matter what the turbulence there, we had no doubt at all about her mother's concern for her daughter and her infant grandson out in such weather. Never mind how riled she must have been before. Never mind how she might react to the news of where Laura and Alan had landed.

We had been casually acquainted with her for years, which somehow made it harder to pick up the phone. But she had to know.

"Laura and Alan are here," I said. "They are going to spend the night."

"Oh, thank God!" she answered.

It wasn't just for the night they stayed, but for nearly a year. Gone was the strain of a teenage mother and an infant living with a grandmother whose health had long been poor. The physical separation gave the psychological unraveling a chance to knit back together.

Years later when Laura dropped in for dinner, she began talking about when she came in to us from the cold. She confided, "Even my mother told me once it was the best thing I ever did."

The longest and most complicated relationship we ever faced was with the mother of David and Roger.

David came to us first, ahead of his brother. Their father was in prison at the time and no one told him where David had gone. Their mother did not want her husband to know; she was angry over David's placement.

She told me that she thought I was trying to take her place.

I asked her once, "Can't we both love him?"

"No. You didn't birth him."

She couldn't help the way she felt, so it was David who wrote to his dad.

David felt exceptionally close to his father. He made plain in his letter how things were at home, how he had met Jack at camp, how he had walked to our house in the night, how his dad was not to worry that we were white.

David showed us the answer, which came quickly. Father told son to take advantage of the significant change in his life.

"It will take courage. Do it for me," he wrote.

After that, they wrote each other nearly every day.

The next step was to arrange a meeting, partly because David's father wanted to know us, but mostly so his son could spend time with him. We delayed the get-together because his mother opposed it, but finally decided she would feel no better about us whether we went or not.

Since David had been placed with us officially, we gained a place on the list of approved visitors. That part was easy. What would it be like when we walked into the prison?

We were directed to an area not unlike an oversized living room, with other family groups talking quietly. A door opened and David's dad came through.

We admitted to each other afterward that for the first minute or two, we were all wound tight with tension. Then we relaxed. We liked him, he liked us and for David it was good. There was only comfort, no tension, in our times together after that.

Home visits could be quite another matter. Foster parents don't need to know—indeed, cannot know—all that goes on in the families from which their youngsters come. Nevertheless, those families need time together, perhaps more than most. So off the kids would go, even in those cases where we knew enough to feel uneasy when they left us for overnight stays.

Most of the time, the gatherings seemed to go well. In fact, the biggest problem on holidays came when birth mom, foster mom and grandma all laid on a feast, and turkeys were not the only items that got stuffed.

Not that real difficulties could always be avoided.

Sometimes youngsters would be absent from the agreed-upon place when it came time for us to pick them up. No one would be home. We would phone grandparents, aunts and uncles until we tracked them down. Why make an issue of it? In a way, this was a divorce. We had no desire to engage in a tug-of-war with the kids in the middle.

They found themselves in the middle of differing expectations all too often.

"When I go home, I can do what I want," lamented one foster son. Since doing what he wanted included not going to school, it took some tactful dialogue to convince him again that this was not an option.

All kids hanker to do what they want; it's what we should expect of them. We knew we should step in when the consequences of "doing what they want" would bring consequences too heavy for them to comprehend.

Some of those we knew who kicked at the traces actually did require time and space away from home so roiling waters might slow again to ripples. Others only needed a sympathetic ear and a return to common sense.

Such was the case with young Jack's friend Kenny, whose misapprehension began with the length of our own lad's hair. That wavy mane reached halfway down Jack's back when he was in high school. We felt uneasy about it, since some people in those hippie times would make assumptions about him that were untrue.

But that was their problem, Jack the Younger pointed out to us. Such a reasonable response settled it: Hair was not a place where we would insist on conformity to our own obviously antiquated tastes.

Enter young Kenny, who came to us and said—this is as close to exactly it as I can remember—"My father made me get my hair cut and I came home and he said to go and get it cut some more and so could I come and live with you?"

"No, dear, just spend the night here and then go home and work it out with him."

If only it had always been so easy.

If only, if only, some of our foster kids had not been so frightfully abused.

10.

Chameleon

CATHY TRIED TO KILL herself twice while living with us. There were also other times when she was committed somewhere.

I came across an old list of things she once asked me to bring her: shampoo and a deck of cards, chocolate milk and a Quarter Pounder. Did I carry them to a locked psychiatric ward? A detoxification center? A state hospital? Or the "tough love" treatment house that finally broke through her pain and shattered the bonds of her chemical addiction?

She was in all of them at one time or another, and what drove her there was a long, harrowing history of abuse by her birth family. In her mid-teens, she wrenched herself away. But the scorn she had known all her life locked her into believing that nothing she did could make her worthy of love.

We could hardly help knowing that Cathy was depressed. She moved through the house like a specter, hardly speaking, rarely smiling. At dinnertime she drifted into the dining room, downed her meal like a nun in cloistered silence and drifted away again.

She dared to show feeling only for Charlie, the cocker spaniel who was hers alone. Like prison inmates who train companion dogs, or like patients in a nursing home when pets come to visit, Cathy found solace in the affection of an animal.

She had learned to keep emotion muffled and to hide what was churning inside.

She wrote a poem about that period. She showed it to me much later. In it, she compared herself to a chameleon, traveling incognito, adapting to change, remaining unknown.

In our bumbling way, we did what we could. We pushed her into counseling. We hugged her when she let us. We watched for signals that she wanted to talk.

When she did crack open the door to feelings, it always seemed to be when I was getting ready to crawl into bed. What to do? Get up and plug in the coffeepot.

One night I made a pot big enough for three. Cathy wanted my youngest daughter, then 17, to sit with us.

"Joan is my sister," she explained.

It didn't dawn on me right away what Cathy was doing: She was saying good-bye. Permanent, I-can't-bear-to-go-on-living good-bye. At age 16.

She was describing hurtful things done to her that we had barely suspected. She was peeling down through layers of pain that we had scarcely perceived.

"I learned to feign immunity to knuckles and boots," she said.

The physical abuse was bad enough; the psychological damage was appalling. Because her mother believed she was possessed by demons, nothing she did could please her parents. She joined school teams because her siblings did. Her parents cheered for them. Never for her. She brought home a straight-A report card. Her mother ground it under her heel; if it was Cathy's, then the devil's hand was in it.

Cathy never said "mother" in our house. Most of the other foster kids used some version of that word for me, whatever felt right. Cathy could not say it, nor could she bring herself to call me "Ann" or "Mrs. Goodwin." So she didn't call me anything. If she answered the phone downstairs and the call was for me, she would come all the way up, find me and tap me on the shoulder.

As she was growing up, only Cathy was branded, not her siblings. They may well have been free to visit upon her any meanness at all.

Cathy was perfectly matter-of-fact in her account to us that night. It was an artful gift: She concealed what she was about to do so that we could later understand it.

Finally, she stubbed out the last in a long succession of cigarettes.

"Good-bye," she said, and walked out of the house. She was oh, so calm.

She had hidden a razor blade in the pocket of her jeans. It was a single-edged blade, one on which she could get a good grip.

I sat frozen, stunned by her suffering. Joan was quicker to catch on.

"Excuse me, Mother," she said, brushing past my chair, and was out the door.

Coming alert at last, I leaped up and flew after them. Mindful that Joan was still fighting a kidney infection, I paused to pluck jackets from hall-closet hangers.

So I lost sight of them.

I headed for the pretty little park where Cathy's troubled soul had sought sanctuary before. Now what she sought was a final end to suffering.

But she had hurried off in the opposite direction. The two teens were nowhere to be seen.

Back home I went, empty jackets in my arms. I woke my husband, who shot outside to pick up the search. I called the police. I summoned any of her older brothers and sisters who still lived nearby. Then I wore a path in the carpet by the phone.

As time dragged on, the police expanded the search to two adjoining suburbs. None of us guessed that Joan and Cathy were locked in a stand-off in a dark field only six blocks away.

Once Cathy had said, "When I mess up, I'll do it alone." What she meant was, "When I die, I'll do it alone."

"Go ahead—kill yourself," Joan challenged.

"I won't do it while you're watching," Cathy retorted.

At one point there was a wrestling match for the razor. The blade dropped to the ground from fingers numbed by temperatures showing the mercury near freezing. Cathy pounced a millisecond sooner.

An hour passed, then two, then four. Neither of them blinked.

Joan, unrecovered from her illness, was blue with cold and shaking in her shirt sleeves. At last Cathy said, "I don't want you to die, too." And so they stumbled home.

I took one look and poured steaming tea. Out came the jackets, of use at last. Soon came a police officer. Ever so gently, he talked Cathy into his squad car and from there to a psychiatric crisis ward.

That was not the only time the police came to our house.

The doorbell rang late one night. Two officers stood on our step, squad car at the curb, red lights flashing.

"Someone in this house is trying to kill herself," they said.

"Oh, no," I said, "you must have the wrong house."

It only took a split second more for me to know. I knew.

"Oh my God, no, you don't have the wrong house."

We raced down to her bedroom. Cathy had swallowed paint thinner.

She had phoned a friend, not really telling, but reluctant, after all, to die alone. Cathy was blurry enough to alarm her confidant, who hung up and dialed for help.

The ambulance was there by the time we got Cathy upstairs. I rode with her to the hospital, as scared as I have ever been.

"If I die tonight," Cathy whispered to me, "I want my mother to have half of what I own."

She paused a moment.

"And I want you to have the other half, plus one penny."

She had another crisis while I was away at a conference. An agitated Cathy lit out from home, with her alert foster sisters, Patti and Laura, right after her.

She hitchhiked.

A young man in a pickup stopped.

Cathy climbed in the cab; the other two leaped in the truck bed behind.

"Where are you going?"

Silence from Cathy.

"We're going where she's going," came from the back.

The young man let them off at a supermarket. Cathy went up and down the aisles, her foster sisters at her heels. They saw her put razor blades in her pocket before she slipped out the door.

She was desperate to get away from them; they were desperate not to lose her. They wrestled her to the ground in a parking lot, screamed for someone to call 911 and sat on Cathy until the police came.

Patti remembers that she had a hunk of Cathy's hair in her hand.

There followed another stay in a psychiatric ward—one more in a series of failed therapies.

There also followed the destruction of a beautiful, doomed dress.

It was a floor-length dress, all cream, with a touch of lace the same soft color around the high neck and barrel cuffs. Cathy looked lovely in it with her fair skin, rosy complexion and dark brown, wavy hair. Patti, a whiz with a needle, had made it for her foster sister to wear to a brother's wedding.

Cathy only got to wear it that one time. After the fearful scene in the parking lot, Patti cut it to pieces and burned it.

"I made that dress for a happy occasion. If Cathy kills herself, I will not see her buried in it," she said.

As Cathy neared her high-school graduation, we thought she had worked her way through her hard times. She made a contract with us, one she had written herself. It covered a legal-pad page and named consequences for every item that she might fail to follow.

"No chemical use" came first. Farther down in the document, she promised not to isolate herself from the family, to be home for supper five nights a week and to ask for what she needed. Some failures would mean she would have to leave us. For less serious infractions, she would be "grounded until you see a change in me."

It told us we were connected. It gave us hope. It got us through to graduation.

But then she moved out on her own and she couldn't hang on. She nosedived into a nightmare of behavior driven by her death-wish.

She cadged drinks from men in bars. In one post-midnight hour, she was so threatened by a man with a switchblade that she called us for rescue. She swallowed Phenobarbital tablets, drank whiskey, passed out, came to, downed more tablets.

"I'd rather die drunk," she told them in the emergency room. She pulled out IVs and they put her in restraints.

The police took her to detoxification units four times in one month. Once she was released from detox and was arrested for being drunk and disorderly later the same day. Another time she plummeted into a two-day blackout.

We signed a probate court order committing her to a state hospital as an "inebriate," a label just one notch more delicate than a "drunk."

A nurse once said to us, "Your daughter is a garbage mouth."

A what?

"Your daughter will take any drug she can get her hands on."

A minister once tried to brace us for what he knew might happen. He cautioned, "No matter how much you care about her, one day one of her suicide attempts could succeed."

Why did we care so much for this teenager, so sore beset? At first it was simply because she was so hopeless, so lost in misery. Then we began to inch past her resistance—her terror, even—of any close relationship. We began to discover her keen mind, quick wit and untapped capacity for affection.

Once she gave me a poem. Now I gave her one of mine:

GEODE
Of course we saw
your skin of rock
that locked you in, alone.
We always knew
a shining core
lay close beneath the stone.

A glimmer of that core broke through when she was placed in a ward with mentally ill adults. She was only 16, but her doctors wouldn't put her in a less-secure adolescent unit because she would neither promise to abandon suicide, nor would she lie about it.

Some patients played cards. Others sat solitary as hermits in the crowded ward. A few shouted, picked quarrels or preached to the air. Aides moved about, keeping peace and parceling out medications.

Just visiting made me edgy. Cathy had to live there for several weeks.

She was the sanest one on the ward. The aides knew it. The patients sensed it: She was the one to whom they passed notes. "Be ready for a breakout," they wrote, or, "I've contacted the police; they're coming to rescue us." She accepted the notes solemnly and tucked them in her sock.

She befriended a bony, white-haired woman she called "Twinkletoes" and entered gently into her delusions. Where was Twinkletoes walking? Where was she flying? Would she teach Cathy to fly?

Finally, Cathy was ready for the adolescent unit, but that treatment program only helped for a while. It wasn't until much later, when she got to Eden House, that the breakthrough came.

Eden House, a "tough love" residential treatment center in Minneapolis, Minnesota, is for hard-core addicts with a long history of chemical addiction and a long record of failure in other treatment programs. In other words, it is for those at the bitter end of a downward spiral. After Eden House, most clients are on their way to recovery, or else they are in prison, or they are dead.

During the 60-day orientation period, new residents are under the rigid control of a primary counselor. About the only thing they get to do without permission is breathe. Every behavior brings reward or penalty.

Clients are isolated from the outside world; we were not allowed to contact Cathy during those two months.

But Eden House contacted us. After two weeks, Cathy had split. Her counselor put us on alert, thinking she might come our way.

We were heartsick.

None of us knew Cathy was on the brink of breakthrough.

After a couple of days on the street, she walked back into Eden House.

Her counselor went nose-to-nose with her: "If you wanted to die, why did you come back?" What could Cathy say to that? After so many years of pain, she faced a hard fact: She wanted to live after all.

"I'll never amount to anything. You are a fool to think so," she cried out once when I shook the bars of her self-imposed prison.

I grabbed her hands hard and spoke of a Cathy who would come to lead a useful life one day, even a happy one. She neither moved nor spoke—nor pulled her hands away.

At last she broke the long silence: "If you can still believe that, maybe I can, too."

She did it. She shattered the bonds of her nightmare past. She found a friend and located in another state. She got a job. She put herself through college. She put herself through law school. She passed the bar exam. She did it.

When she came to the house to see me before she moved out of Minnesota, she gave me her picture, quite casually, keeping it light.

"Let's have lunch before I leave," she said. "My treat," she added.

Then at the door, at the last moment, she leaned across and kissed me. She kissed me of her own accord, this young woman who, in early days with us, had flinched, drawn sharp breath and gone rigid when we reached out to stroke or hug her.

Now she was ready for life on her own.

In the place where she would be living, she could not take her cocker spaniel. He whimpered when the door closed behind her.

Not me. Not for this good-bye.

11.

Pomp and Circumstances

I, WHO NEVER IRON anything, claimed the proud, symbolic privilege of pressing a gratifying parade of high-school graduation gowns.

David's grandmother and I shared tissues as we perched high in the bleachers on his appointed day. She and I put a good dent in the box after she told me he was the first in his family to finish high school. Even at a distance, it was easy for us to pick our boy out of the blue-clad line. His was the one black face.

No wonder our graduates stir up such emotion. We well know their past struggles. We have seen them through spelling tests and term papers, pop quizzes and lab reports. We have fretted over more serious matters like incompletes and lost credits. Now we can only guess at the hazards that lie ahead, hazards they will go on to face without us.

The opening bars of "Pomp and Circumstance" signal "finale" to their dependence. We sit in the bleachers, harboring the bittersweet hope that they are ready to leave us behind. No wonder the throat constricts when the name for which we wait comes winging to our ear.

The famous "Pomp" processional comes with words I treasure. Choked up though I was on David's day, I did not remain silent as the band played it the first time through. "Land of hope and glory," I warbled softly, "mother of the free."

I had already given my best to "The Star Spangled Banner," high notes and all. With most others joining in the anthem, I felt comfortable belting that baby out.

At the dinner table once, one of our boys asked me what I planned to do with my time when I didn't have so many kids. "I'm going to take singing lessons," I said, not missing a beat.

"Mom, do you have a lot of money?" he shot back, to general merriment.

Well! I just wish they could have heard my rendition of the National Anthem at a ball game some time later. A man in the row ahead turned around and observed, "Lady, there must be church choirs all over this country looking for you." I chose to take it as a compliment.

So I sang the anthem with gusto at this graduation, where the black and white people who loved David best had gathered as one family. Together we watched a long line of young men and women march onto the field with measured dignity.

They looked great in their caps and gowns.

Someone announced awards and the audience signaled approval. Someone made a speech the audience would scarcely remember. Then into each youthful hand came a precious piece of parchment bearing a few words in fancy script. It was for this that the audience had come.

When it was over, the newly graduated shed their solemn dignity along with their matching robes and tasseled mortarboards. Soon enough, they would be taking their turn at the helm of this land of hope and glory. Now it was time to party.

That night, David and four others of our brood piled into the roomiest of the family cars. They revealed to us later that one of them took to mooning out a rear window.

A policeman pulled them over. He asked them for their names and addresses, one after the other. With perfect truth, each supplied the same address with a different last name. Turning to the fifth and final teen, the officer observed, "I suppose you live at #4657, too."

"Oh, Mom, I was so scared he would think we were smarting off," Nancy told me later. But he didn't doubt, or else he didn't mind. He well knew it was graduation night.

"Stay cool, kids" was all he said. That's my kind of cop.

In the graduation line-up a few years later, it was Joan's and Laura's turn. Joan was college-bound but Laura, already with a son to support, would not get the life she had once imagined—the college years with the art major.

Instead, what lay ahead were rented quarters so cramped that the closet offered the only space for Alan's crib. What awaited was work as a nurse's aide on the late-night shift so Alan could sleep at his grandmother's house.

Dollars would not stretch to include babysitting during the day, so Laura fenced Alan in while she dozed on the couch. She never asked for welfare help until he started school, and then just enough for latch-key care so she could juggle work schedules and nursing classes.

Often she felt overcome with exhaustion. But there was Alan, who said, "It'll be all right, Mom." The first time he voiced that, he was not yet 3 years old.

She never stopped studying until she added "R.N." to her name.

Along the way, she married. We danced all the way to her wedding and sang all the way home.

There's a Chinese proverb that says, "Keep a green tree in your heart and perhaps a singing bird will come." To this day, Laura laughs much, copes gamely and expects the singing bird.

12.

It's All in the Genes

A LONG TIME AGO in Ireland, my grandparents invited a distant relative to spend a week or two in their home. She stayed three years. The only reason she left was because she died.

A couple of generations later, I lived with my family outside Washington, D.C. during my formative years. Everybody eventually goes to Washington, and many of the friends my parents made in the several countries where they had lived landed on our doorstep at one time or another. People were floating in and out of our house all the time.

That took on enlarged dimensions during World War II. We were located near the military bases at Annapolis, Maryland, and Quantico, Virginia. During periods when my brother was stationed at one and my brother-in-law at the other, weekend passes meant open house at our address for their comrades-in-training who were far from home.

The young sailors and Marines seized the rare chance to sleep in, of course, some of them for most of the morning. And, of course, they woke up hungry.

I claimed the task of chief waffle-maker. After all, that role had been mine every Sunday morning on a smaller scale since I was old enough to measure flour.

The servicemen who surfaced first declared themselves ready for more by the time the sleepyheads had appeared, pulled up to the table and taken their turn. Thus a minor mountain of waffles disappeared, week after week.

Our neighbors took pity and shared ration coupons for sugar and butter.

How unkind it would be to carry on about such a breakfast treat and fail to share the recipe. It's so simple that even I, from my earliest and most awkward adolescence, couldn't goof it up:

GOOF-PROOF WAFFLES
> 2 cups flour
> 2 teaspoons baking powder
> 2 tablespoons sugar
> ½ teaspoon salt
> 2 eggs, beaten
> 2 cups milk
> 6 tablespoons melted butter

Sift first four ingredients together.
Combine eggs and milk. Add to flour mixture.
Fold in melted butter.

Keep making batches until all those present declare themselves F.F.T.B.—(family code for Full Fit to Bust).

Feeding the young men who spent so many weekends with us was simple, compared to providing them with beds. We needed ones that folded up—a commodity hard to find in wartime Washington. My resourceful Mum scoured the town by telephone and then scurried after anything flat with four legs that could be squished down for storage during the week.

Suppose you were a visitor in those days. You gained an advantage by arriving early, because you would enjoy a wider choice of sleeping accommodations. Unlucky you, should you bring up the rear in the march to the house: You had to slip gingerly into the bed with the wobbly legs. Unless you turned over carefully, it could, and did, collapse amidships, folding you inside itself.

Either that, or you were allotted for the night the malevolent lightweight that rose up and bonked you on the back of the head, should you thoughtlessly sit down on the foot-end to shed your shoes.

Looking over the motley choices as the house filled up, my father announced that he reserved one right: He was going to sleep in his own bed with his own wife. Mum, all too mindful of the rickety cots, made no objection.

And so by blind luck and accident of birth, I came from a welcoming tradition. I lived under circumstances that abundantly provided food and affection. Only a clod could fail to appreciate basking in such warmth. Only an ingrate would turn from those shivering in the chill.

Long before I knew my husband, he had his own close encounter with the ins and outs of home-sharing. When he was a teenager, a cousin of like age needed temporary shelter. Jack's parents came forward.

The boys made up a baseball game with trading cards, which they played endlessly. They also invented a game they called "Battleship." Too bad they didn't patent that one, because somebody eventually came up with essentially the same idea and put it on the market. It is still sold today, including pricey electronic versions.

On summer mornings the two boys toiled together, hoeing the huge garden that helped to feed the family. Free in the afternoons, they took off to find adventure in a nearby forest preserve.

"Temporary shelter" stretched into a three-year stay. Jack's sister and the two boys all squeezed into one bedroom in their small house in the country, a blanket hung mid-room for privacy. Crowded? Yes, with pleasant memories.

My father-in-law was a gentle, scholarly man with a quiet way of helping others. In the 35 years that he lived after I married his son, I came to know and love his worth.

When he died, the family embarked on the bittersweet, memory-tugging task of sorting through his belongings.

One thing puzzled us. We found dollar bills in his suit jackets, overcoats and cardigans. Not just any old dollar bills, but nice, crisp, new ones, there in a handy pocket of every outer garment.

We were only baffled until we reflected what a kind and generous person he had been. It was his habit to take daily walks along the streets of the city where he lived. We concluded that he kept those bills where he could get at them easily, if anyone should ask for money.

I thought of that in the wake of a miserable little incident awhile back when my husband and I were visiting relatives in New York City. We had occasion there to take a bus from the Port Authority, that immense, bustling terminal in the middle of Manhattan.

As we stood in line to buy tickets, I felt a touch on my shoulder. A shriveled little man was standing there, hand held out to us. The palm of the hand was cracked. His hair stood in wisps around a thin and graying face. I don't suppose he weighed a hundred pounds.

"Could I have some change, so I could get something to eat?" he asked.

We fumbled around in our pockets but we weren't quick enough. The ticket-seller, waving his arms as one would to shoo away an annoying insect, yelled at the wretched little person loudly enough to attract a passing policeman.

The officer ordered him up against the wall.

"But I ain't done nothin'," the man protested, in a voice as reedy as himself. In the next dizzying seconds, the policeman took the man down to the floor, snapped handcuffs on him and hauled him to his feet. Then the two were gone, swallowed up in the anonymous crowd.

"I ain't done nothin'," the man wailed. He was right. He hadn't done anything—and neither had we. We had kept no kindly bill in a ready pocket. We had spoken no moderating word to the arresting officer. We had just stood there as the harsh little scene played out, our jaws dropped, looking like the rubes from the country that we were.

We spoke no word. I don't suppose it would have made any difference if we had. They've got laws to keep shriveled little men at a distance from folks like ourselves, born under luckier stars. It wouldn't have made any difference.

Still, I'm glad my father-in-law wasn't there to see it.

There's no question: Jack the Elder grew up with those who shared.

There's also no question: It's in the genes, this mind-set of ours that meant we were ready when the foster kids began to trickle in.

As Jack and I made a life together, a couple of added factors came into play. One was the birth of our first child. As that new life slid into the world, I was overcome with a sense of wonder and a surge of love astonishing in its intensity.

All my life, I'd been a casual church-goer. This did it; this birth sent me to my knees. It's common knowledge that Mother Nature ordains such deep-felt gratitude for a child; never mind; it overwhelmed me and I never got over it.

Time sped by, two more babies appeared and the second factor kicked in. As our children and their friends grew up, Jack and I realized how much we liked teenagers. We enjoyed their high spirits, appreciated their honesty, admired their courage.

Even so, we didn't consciously set out to become foster parents. It never occurred to us to rise from the breakfast table, or pause while brushing our teeth, or pull over on the way to work to ask each other, "Don't we have an empty bed some-place? Shouldn't we find somebody to fill it?"

It was more simple, more natural, than that: One fateful night, when the genes and the mind-set were in line with the stars, a desperate David threw pebbles at a window. That deed set off a ripple powerful enough to wash teen-agers onto our shores for the 10 years that were to come.

Even after that interval passed, there always seemed to be at least one non-relative in residence.

For years, we housed actors from the local community the-ater. Once, we put in a security system that caused a deal of trouble because the cats kept setting it off. Before we knew it, the nice young man who came repeatedly to adjust it was living in our basement. It seemed like the practical thing.

When he moved in, we needed to change our phone mes-sage. The fresh one began, "This is the home of Ann, Jack and Jason." We had forgotten to mention our newest resident to Jack the Younger, by that time living half a continent away.

He called later. "Have I got a new brother, and you never told me?"

Today, if I stop at a table in a restaurant to discuss the soup with a stranger, my husband will whisper on the way out, "When is she coming to live with us?"

He's joking, of course.

I think.

13.
Sensible Shoes

MOST OF THE TEENAGERS who stumbled through our door came with as many bruises as if they had plummeted headlong down a flight of stairs, except that they wore their bruises on the inside.

It was one thing for them to find us, or for us to find them. But troubled behavior is all too likely after the kind of hurt they had endured.

Friends who knew us well understood how Jack the Elder and I could have been ready to take in teens as they came along. But they wondered: When those youngsters made major mistakes, did we always agree on what to do?

We did.

We already knew that the one essential about parenting was to care about your children, and to show it. We embraced the wisdom of logical consequences, even though we had not yet learned to call them that. We did not believe in spanking, slapping or striking a youngster of any age in any way.

In the interests of full disclosure, I must reveal that on one occasion I paddled our eldest daughter. Nancy was about

4 years old when she and her little friend Mimi embarked on an adventure. They wandered a couple of blocks from home, where their frantic mothers found them later, munching on crackers—sitting on railroad tracks.

The unaccustomed spanking that followed had the intended effect. Decades later, Nancy, her gentle nature unchanged by the chastisement, has neither wandered about irresponsibly nor been run over by a train.

Jack the Elder agreed, as I knew he would: The situation called for sterner measures than a talking-to and a time-out.

Our daughter Joan calls her Dad and me "the parental unit." She's got that right; her words describe the depth of understanding between us.

The best example of how in tune we are came in March 1965, in a two-sentence conversation that became the defining moment of our marriage.

One night back then, Jack the Elder and I watched a movie on television, the heart-tugging "Diary of Anne Frank."

The next night, we watched the news, as was our custom. A police dog tore the clothes off a man as, terrified, he tried to get away. A policeman turned a high-pressure water jet on a woman, the force of it knocking her over and rolling her down the street. The woman was no bigger than my tiny mother.

Their crime, to provoke such a response? Registering to vote in Selma, Alabama—or, more accurately, trying to register. The would-be voters? American citizens like me, except that they were black.

It didn't take long for me to make the connection. Would I, could I have done anything to protest the deadly oppression of Jews in Germany in the early days of the Nazi menace, when Jews began to lose their rights, and then their lives? I wasn't there. I don't know.

But this was my America, and the hideously wrong thing that was happening was in the now.

I turned to Jack and said, "I want to go to Selma."

He answered in the next instant, "Of course you should go, if that's what you have to do."

So I put on my sensible shoes and went to Selma.

We couldn't have known then that Viola Liuzzo, a housewife like me, a mother like me, would go there like me—and would be killed, forced off the road one night and then shot in the head because her car had out-of-state license plates and she was white and she had a black person in her car.

But we did have sense enough to know that I might be putting myself in some degree of danger. How could I do that to my children?

Ah, but that's just the point. I didn't do it to my children. I did it for them.

I heard of an Episcopal priest who was flying to Selma the next day with four more clergymen in collars. So I laced up those shoes, put a simple, silver cross around my neck and joined them, leaving behind a husband somewhat less worried, given the company I was in.

Little did we realize that any person in clerical garb would be the object of special scorn in Selma. "Where'd you get the priest suit?" was a frequent taunt on the day we marched.

After all, we were in the Bible Belt. The church-going people there could not bring themselves to believe that ordained persons would do what we were doing, would come from all over the nation to protest their vote-denying strategies, would attract a following army of reporters and photographers to expose their problems to all the world. They simply could not see the sin and error in their horrendous treatment of their fellow Americans.

But that's getting ahead of the story.

I remember peeling carrots for my family's dinner that last evening before I left, acutely aware that I would be leaving my husband to take over so many such daily tasks, wondering at the same time where my own meals would be coming from for the next few days.

I need hardly have worried about that. The black people of Selma opened their hearts to us, hundreds upon hundreds of us, feeding us and housing us and joining in the march, often in fact and always in spirit.

How could I ever forget the name of the woman who took me in? She was Martha Washington. When I came back to her after a night under arrest, she rushed out to me. "I wanted to bring you a blanket," she cried, "but I didn't know how to get it to you."

But that's getting ahead of the story.

The morning after I arrived, worried civil rights leaders called all those who were gathering in Selma into Brown Chapel. The chapel had become unofficial headquarters for the march, scheduled to begin a couple of days later.

Our leaders and strategists included towering names in the civil rights movement, among them Dr. Martin Luther King, Jr., and Dr. Ralph Bunche, both already winners of the Nobel Peace Prize.

And John Lewis, who earlier in Selma had been beaten so brutally by police that his skull was fractured. How soul-stirring it is to note that 22 years later, Lewis walked into the U.S. Capitol in Washington, D.C., a duly elected congressman from Georgia.

There was ample reason for worry, a leader explained. Earlier, two of our group had walked into a part of town where only white people lived, hoping to encounter some who would talk with them.

They were arrested and disappeared into the Selma jail.

Unlike Alice, who tumbled out of sight down the rabbit hole into adventure, these two had fallen straight into peril. In Selma in 1965, the possibility of brutal treatment for protesters was all too real.

So the plan was for as many of us who would, should walk where they had walked. We would go two by two, since we did not yet have a parade permit.

Those who went were likely to be arrested.

Off we set, ferried there by car in relays, about 700 of us. I don't remember the exact number, but it was at least that; we counted off when we had a chance to do it later in the day.

We went two-by-two on our non-parade, each pair well-separated from the couple ahead. When my turn came, off I started with a partner who told me his name was Tom Paine. Maybe he just wanted it to be, but I hope it really was.

A line of police officers waited for us down the block.

Getting arrested in Selma was the easiest thing in the world. As we two approached, a policeman asked, "Are y'all with this movement?"

I remember he was running his hand up and down his billy club.

"Yes, sir, we are," I answered.

"You're under arrest. Get on that bus."

I looked him in the eye. I smiled at him. Then Tom Paine, my little silver cross and I climbed up the three or four steps of the bus.

The police needed that bus and more besides. Every one of us was arrested.

We were taken to a community center. We stood in rows in a central courtyard for an hour or so, men, women and some black children with their parents. No one was allowed to speak or to sit down. No one was allowed to make a phone call, despite repeated requests.

Then we were ordered to go inside the building. After herding us in, the police consulted outside. We did the same on the inside.

Once alone, we counted off. After that, our leaders correctly predicted what would happen.

Chief of Police Eugene "Bull" Connor came in and told us we had not been arrested after all. I can't recall his exact words, but he indicated that it had all been just a mistake. Why didn't we just go back up north, or wherever it was we had come from?

But we had broken no law and we had, in fact, been arrested. We would make the protest we had agreed upon while we were left to ourselves: We would spend the night in the community center.

We had the option of leaving the building while we could. Only one among us did, and that reluctantly; he needed to travel back home for a commitment he could not break.

The chief reddened in anger when he heard our plan, because the situation was rapidly becoming a public-relations disaster. He fumed at us that he would take all protection away from the center.

That's exactly what he did. We listened to rebel yells and saw the headlights of cars circling the building all night.

We women took the children to the recreation hall upstairs and settled them for the night as best we could. I remember that a pool table lined with sweaters became a makeshift bed. The men barricaded the doors downstairs with whatever they could find.

It was a long night. But I had my cross, and I knew this by heart from the Book of Common Prayer:

> O Lord, support us all the day long,
>   until the shadows lengthen and the evening comes,
>   and the busy world is hushed, and the fever of life is
> over,
>   and our work is done.
> Then in thy mercy grant us
>   a safe lodging, and a holy rest, and peace at the last.
> Amen.

Next morning, we walked back through white Selma to our black homes, moving silently through a gauntlet of jeering people. It was our intent to do nothing that would provoke violence. Thankfully, there was none.

But that's when I first heard, "Where'd you get the priest suit?"

On the first day of the march to Montgomery, Alabama's capital, we all walked about seven miles. We numbered somewhere between 7,000 and 8,000 by then. Volunteer marshals, our fellow protesters, kept us moving and quiet. Helicopters buzzed overhead. Police were everywhere, but none seemed inclined to put their billy clubs to use.

I felt exhilarated. Despite bystanders shouting hateful things, I didn't feel the least bit frightened, unlike that night in the community center.

However, we would not have been safe along the route at night. That is why all but about 300 of us did what the leaders asked and took whatever wheels came along to carry us back to town.

One woman told me that as she settled into the back seat of the first available car, the man who got in beside her put out his hand and introduced himself.

"How do you do?" he said. "My name is Ralph Bunche."

It was indeed he of the Nobel Peace Prize.

Had she known that he would go on to become Undersecretary-General of the United Nations, and would receive the Presidential Medal of Honor, the Presidential Medal of Freedom and more than 30 honorary degrees, she might not have been able to stammer out any reply at all.

Those who walked the whole 54 miles from Selma to the capital camped along the way, heavily guarded. The march took five days.

What a spirit-lifter it must have been to be in camp the last night! Somebody put together a makeshift stage for an array of stars, come to do the marchers honor: Harry Belafonte, Tony Bennett, Frankie Laine, Sammy Davis, Jr., and Peter, Paul and Mary among them.

At the final rally at the Alabama Capitol the next day, the crowd had swelled to an estimated 25,000, there to petition with one accord for the protection of black registrants.

I could not wait it out to get to Montgomery for the thrill of that concluding event. After the first day on the road, I went home to my family—just before Viola Liuzzo was murdered. For my husband's sake, I am grateful for that.

In church on my first Sunday home, one friend said, "You carried the cross for me in Selma." Tears well at the memory.

I shall always be glad that I was there.

Five months later, President Lyndon B. Johnson signed the Voting Rights Act of 1965.

I did it for my children.

And because my husband, in tune as always, understood that I had to.

14.
Balance Sheet

WHEN THEY WERE IN high school, David and Jack the Younger worked out a nightly routine that seldom wavered. First they made sandwiches. After an hour or so, they fixed popcorn. Once in awhile they varied that by baking chocolate chip cookies.

Finally, each poured himself a mound of cereal and floated it in milk. For this, David used a vegetable serving dish, not one of those skimpy bowls most folks choose for their shredded wheat.

This all came after they had polished off a hearty dinner.

While they indulged their nightly ritual, I honored my weekly one. Off I would go to the supermarket, where I was familiar with the location of nearly every item, especially the cereal boxes. It took two grocery carts to handle the usual supplies. I would fill one cart, leave it up front by the cashier and start loading another until it, too, was brimming.

I'm convinced the manager did a little dance when I pulled in the parking lot: "Yesssss! In the black another week!" For all I know, he pushed a bell that rang in corporate headquarters, to set the CEO a-dancing, too.

Surely he danced on the weekends we went camping. In the fresh air around an open fire, our eating machines outdid themselves. On one crisp morning, six of them went through four pound-and-a-half loaves of bread making French toast.

Sometimes folks ask about the costs of having all those kids.

If they mean money, well, the fridge was never locked.

When we gave out allowances, everybody got the age-related same.

When a foster daughter needed glasses, we saw dozens of frames on a wall rack, displayed in row upon gleaming row. But we soon learned that these were not for such as her. At the words "welfare client," the clerk abruptly thrust into her hands a box with a few, a very few, jumbled and unattractive choices. Our daughter quietly deemed them "dorky." She was right.

Who would send a young person to school in something that made her feel dorky?

Six of our foster kids stayed with us under a loose, often uneasy agreement with their parents. The other seven were "official," placed in our home by the county. For the latter, the county reimbursed us.

We thought the rates reasonable, certainly enough to cover decent food, clothing and a minimum of extras. But I can't imagine foster parents coming out ahead.

Sometimes when people bring up costs, the question is more profound; they mean personal wear and tear.

What did the swelling family census do to our biological trio?

Nancy was 17 when the first foster kid came, her sights set on college a little less than a year away, an old hand at big-sisterhood. We didn't really worry about negative impacts on her.

Young Jack was 16, nearly—but not quite—through the rocky shoals of adolescence. We worried some about him.

Joan was only 12. We worried about Joan.

Joan says now that when the foster kids were treading troubled waters, parental love stretched thin. It was there, she says. But thin.

Her brother adds, "Because other needs were more immediate, sometimes it seemed that mine were less important."

There were costs to them.

There were costs to my husband and me. We stewed more and slept less, according to the sum total of adolescents in residence. How could we meet so many needs when we hardly knew what some of them were?

Actually, deep down we did know. They needed what we all do: someone to listen, to accept, sometimes to steer, always to care.

While the worries could be monumental, ah, so were the rewards.

Consider the time Joan and Cathy had the stand-off over the razor blade. Joan has said, "I grew up that night. For the first time, I had a sense of mortality: Somebody my age might die. Could die. Here. Tonight.

"For the first time, I knew that sometimes you have to take responsibility for another human being."

Nancy has said, "For Jack and me as older teens, the suburbs could be boring. It was just more fun to have lots of other kids around. Besides, we didn't live in a white ghetto anymore."

What she expressed, she also drew. A card she made showed a teen crew gathered for her father's birthday, all grinning, including her two richly brown-skinned brothers. It said inside:

> Papa's days are filled with joys
> from all his little girls and boys.
> Some are his and some are not;
> Just look at all the joys you got.

As for Jack the Younger's final judgment of our elastic household, he once told us, "I would do it again with my eyes open."

And then there was the message he sent to be read at his dad's retirement party: "When I learned that my father was retiring after 40 years on a newspaper, it got me thinking, and I realized that for all employees who had been there 39 years or less, my father had always been there That amazed me. I didn't understand how he could be in two places at once, because he was always there for me, too."

More than once he also exclaimed, "Well! You wouldn't give me a brother, so I had to go out and get my own!"

Yet it wasn't always easy.

One weekend, David and Jack attended a teen retreat. The advance information read, "Do your own thing," so the boys packed up their drum set—the works: kettle, bass, snare, cymbals, top hat. They had a thundering good time; at least the campers did, although possibly not the counselors.

Then David got out of line and Jack pulled him back. That's all we know. We heard only the fact, stripped of details.

A retreat leader collared me soon after, concerned about the weight Jack carried as big brother. I told him that like true siblings, the boys didn't always get along.

David once complained, "You say you wanted a brother. I do what you want, but you won't do what I want to do."

Jack answered, "I'm new at this brother bit. Give me a chance."

They were working out their problems on their own. When the retreat leader heard that, he figured both boys were doing just fine.

Our son's English teacher once asked her students to identify their favorite passage from literature. The fact that some of his siblings were black may have influenced Jack's choice, the dramatic moment when Huckleberry Finn remembers floating down the Mississippi with Jim. A runaway slave, Jim is the closest thing to a loving father that Huck will ever know.

Huck muses that Jim "would always call me honey, and pet me, and do everything he could think of for me, and how good he always was."

Yet the adults in Huck's world are blind to Jim's goodness and affection. If they had known Huck was harboring this "nigger," this sub-human, this piece of property, they would have scorned the boy and promised him descent to everlasting fire.

Huck teeters on the brink of betraying Jim back into slavery.

He can't do it. Against all he has been taught, his better nature triumphs.

Says Huck to himself, "All right, then, I'll go to hell."

And that's the literary moment Jack the Younger loves best.

Jack described his foster-brother role in a college application. He wrote, "The experience that has had the biggest influence on my outlook came when my parents took into my family David, a black friend of mine whose father and older brother were in prison and whose mother, through problems of her own, could not provide a good home for him.

"Many problems arose as we all learned to live together. David confided in me more easily than in my parents; my parents asked my help in understanding him.

"Through experiences with David and his family, I gained a firsthand knowledge of such urgent problems as prison reform, administration of welfare funds, child neglect and juvenile probation.....I don't have any ready solutions to those problems, but I realize how complex they are and how important it is to care about them."

Young Jack hadn't told us about his chosen topic. He just flipped the application on the dining room table one night and said, "Here. I thought you'd like to read this."

Jack the Elder and I count the changes in our three birth-children as abundant compensation for occasional chaos. They will never be the same.

Neither will we.

We two also gained new regard for friends and neighbors, whose kindness and understanding never chilled as some of our newcomers only gradually let go of their old survival skills of lying and stealing.

We gained intensity in our prayer lives: The good Lord saw to it that we never lacked for subjects.

We gained an elevated capacity for patience: The good Lord knew we needed it.

We gained awareness: While powerless to tackle global problems, we could touch single lives.

We gained the role of proud witnesses, over and over, as our kids eased into adult lives. I remember beaming at a nervous Patti at her first political caucus, drafting a resolution and seeing it pass.

We gained walls crammed with photos: Jack the Younger juggling a book, a bottle and baby Alan as he boned up for a class. Roger hugging Pooh Bear, our Samoyed puppy, brown hands buried in fluffy white fur. Patti in wig and clown suit, staging a party for retarded teens. Laura at her spinning wheel, waist-length hair falling over her shoulders. Joan beaming approval at Tania in her scarlet graduation gown.

How do the foster teens themselves weigh the balance?

Cathy told us that when she first lived with us, she kept waiting for my husband to smack me, or for one or the other of us to strike her. She thought family life was like that.

She, who once recoiled at an adult hand reaching for her, learned to endure, and then return, a kiss. She wrote a friend, "It's hard to hug in a straitjacket."

She, who once held herself rigidly apart from our family life, insisted on making the morning coffee when she visited, and then used her carpentry skills to make household repairs we klutzy parents hadn't figured out how to do.

At one time she developed a game for children who receive social services, encouraging them to tally the good they do every day: "I share my toys," for instance. "I help my mom." "I don't make fun of others." "I do my chores."

And, "I'm a good person."

She wrote us that she wants children to know that abuse is never deserved and feeling worthwhile is unconditional. She ended her letter, "If giving love is a parent's job, then you're my real Mom and Dad."

After Cathy moved to the West Coast, the intervals between our letters and phone calls gradually grew longer. I told myself that we were busy and she was busy. Suddenly, that felt like an excuse

You would think she had gone to the moon.

One day I realized with dismay that we had lost track of her. I backed away from attempts at reconnecting for a cowardly reason: I quailed at the idea of calling her parents, the only way I could think of to trace her. They had been less than pleased when she came to live with us.

Finally I just did it. I picked up the phone. Her mother gave me Cathy's number.

That's how we made the proud discovery of what she had been up to, supporting herself while earning college and law degrees. She passed the bar exam on the first try, which fewer than half the test-takers typically do. Then she flew out to see us with her diploma tucked in her suitcase. It read, "cum laude."

All this she had wrung from the darkness of her early life. The brightness of the moment when we held her diploma in our hands was the finest gift she could have given to a pair of proud foster parents.

There are other gifts.

Laura made us a fringed rug, striped in smoky blue and creamy white. The wool came from her own flock of llamas, sheep and angora goats; the dyeing, spinning and weaving from her own hand.

Alan made us a wobbly stool with sticks for legs when he was old enough to go to summer camp. I keep meaning to paint "The End" on it.

Cathy gave us James Herriott's book, "All Things Bright and Beautiful." In the flyleaf, she wrote that it should be titled "Most Things Bright and Beautiful," because we weren't in it.

Steve once remarked, "A fellow can't have too many moms." He and his wife Lynda made me god-mom to their first baby.

At David's wedding reception, his bride pinned flowers on Jack and me, so other guests would know we were family. We would not have traded those posies for a queen's crown jewels.

One of our presents to the newlyweds was the same voluminous vegetable dish from which the bridegroom had once devoured his after-dinner cereal snack. We didn't care whether it matched their tableware and neither did they.

Patti, who sewed and destroyed the dress for Cathy, made a white crepe blouse for me, embroidering the bodice with delicate flowers of petal pink and soft maroon. One of these years I shall be buried in it. Funerals don't wring the heart when a person has had a good run. Patti won't need to burn that blouse.

She painted us a card once—we could stock a store with handmade cards. The outside sported a green wash of watercolor with splashes of blue, red and yellow. The inside read, "My life is better because you incourage (sic) me to try." She went on to become a teacher, and then a teacher of teachers, who even learned to spell.

Patti never drifted away. Of those who did, some have drifted back.

After a long absence, Bill called us—he of the pie tins under the bed. A phone ad that urged "Reach out and touch someone" had triggered his welcome impulse.

It's been ages since we've heard from Tania. We keep the telephone plugged in.

In worrisome times, healing waves came washing over us from beyond the home shores. When Cathy plunged into choppy seas, a prayer cycle in our church kick-started into emergency mode. A sheet went the rounds and people signed up for every hour, night and day, to petition for her safety. Beside one post-midnight slot, four names appeared.

The praying circle widened beyond our congregation. Cathy's teachers signed up, as did her friends. Our friends. Our neighbors. The woman who cuts my hair. All on their knees at one time or another until Cathy found her way home.

Al Shaff, my fellow teacher, left us money in his will to buy extra treats for the kids. We savored the gesture and were pleased to forego the treats; the man is still on the planet.

Still the ripples come.

When Patti had gone on to her own teaching career, she invited me to visit her middle-school class in an inner-city school. There, she introduced me as her foster mother.

"Ohhhhhh!" Students pounced on teacher. "What did you do to be bad?"

It came as news to many of them that you don't have to "be bad" to be in a foster home. It came as a connection between an instructor and some of her disadvantaged students.

We see Patti doing splendidly, and others, too: Steve. Laura. Alan. Cathy. Nancy, Jack and Joan, the three originals.

What of the rest? Are they all right, out on their own? We don't know, for sure. So what we do is hope.

In a swirling 10-year span, we watched our kids help each other. We witnessed their saving humor, their compassion and their capacity to share.

There's no denying that sometimes the down side loomed large. When our foster kids stumbled, we came to know assistant principals, police officers and chemical dependency counselors. We saw the inside of detox units and locked psychiatric wards.

A few of those young people did terrible things to escape their pain: They took drugs, they drank, they tried to kill themselves. Yet they found the courage to seek a safe harbor with adults they scarcely knew. We call that bright and beautiful.

And brave. Especially brave.

Epilogue
Grown. Some Gone.

WHERE ARE THEY NOW, those who once slept downstairs?

THE THREE ORIGINALS
Nancy, mother of our only grandchild, is a nurse at a medical clinic in a residence for troubled boys in upstate New York. (She had known a few; who is surprised at the direction of her career?)

Jack the Younger was music director of the New York Choral Society for 25 years. Now he appears as guest conductor with various choruses.

Joan, a neuropsychologist, is a professor of clinical neurology and psychiatry at a New England hospital, and is board-certified in her specialty.

All three of our children are happily married.

THE 13 WHO FOLLOWED
Cathy, who once recoiled from human touch and was so perilously suicidal, became an attorney working as an advocate for the disadvantaged, the abused and the mentally ill.

Patti served for two years in the Peace Corps, where she said she went, not to teach children to read, but to teach them to love to read. She continued this work that she was born to do in Louisiana public schools. Recently retired, she creates work for sale in leather, stained glass and fabric.

Steve Brandt, who rose to my defense in his high-school journalism classroom, worked for decades as a distinguished reporter for the *Star Tribune* in Minneapolis and is also recently retired. He is the father of our godson and of another son who is our godson-in-spirit.

Laura, who swept in out of the storm with infant Alan, is a staff nurse in the psychiatric emergency ward of a county medical center. With her husband, she owns and operates a fiber farm with upwards of 200 llamas, alpacas, sheep and angora goats; she spins, weaves and knits. I suppose she finds time to sleep.

Alan, now a man grown, is an elections specialist, programming machines that count ballots and creating the ballots themselves. With his wife, he is renovating a century-old house.

David, our first arrival, is a construction worker. We are in and out of touch.

"Pie-Tin Bill" did not call again. We knew one another very little, and the contact withered away.

Roger, the little brother, was murdered.

Daniel, who slept in the Salvation Army drop-box, died accidentally when struck by a softball.

We have lost touch with four others:

* with Tania, who wasted no time claiming the prized basement bedroom;

* with Wayne, who disappeared amongst the art-museum masterpieces;

* with Stanley, who skipped classes and shirked chores; and

* with Karla, who settled in briefly and drifted away.

Postscript
One Child at a Time

REMOVING A CHILD FROM a fractured home is like extracting a tooth broken at the root. Both are preceded by pain and accomplished with difficulty.

The courts make it hard to pull children from their parents. It should be.

Sometimes it must be done.

Or sometimes a family is plunged into such distress—by devastating illness, for example—that dismayed parents may not, for a time, be able to care for their children.

So where are these children to go? Foster homes are one answer, but there are rarely enough of them.

Let's suppose, let's hope, that you are moved to offer such a home. How to begin?

Check out "AdoptUSKids," a national resource that discusses the steps a family would go through on the way to foster or adoptive care.

Get in touch with a local county social service agency (check the phone book) to get local advice on what your next move should be. Ask the people there to explain requirements, such as a background check and a home safety inspection.

Then ask to begin the process.

Then be ready to embark on one of the most challenging, the most rewarding, the most important journeys you will ever undertake.

Acknowledgments

STRESSED ADOLESCENTS TORE OUR hearts, but gladdened them far more.

Thanks be to the 13.

Like a trio of retrievers, our own three fetched several floundering youngsters safely onto shore and then helped them fit into their new family.

Thanks be to the three.

Jack the Elder, who helps me accomplish what my heart leads me to do, did it again with this book.

Thanks be to the husband.

Professionals, more in number than I know, guided our brood through calm and storm alike. They include Mike Kennedy, that wisest of probation officers; teachers, counselors and administrators in School District 281, Robbinsdale, Minnesota; and staff members of a string of adolescent crisis units, detox centers, juvenile detention facilities, state hospitals and the like.

Thanks be to the professionals.

Numerous friends never wavered in their understanding and support, even when our kids' occasional misdeeds bruised their shins as well as our own. Mary and Don Roening and Karen Bowen lead that long black-and-blue roll of honor.

Thanks be to these friends.

As work on the book proceeded all too slowly, I stumbled happily upon a retreat for writers and artists in Lake Forest, Illinois. I accomplished much of the writing during several sessions in that place, so full of serenity and support.

Thanks be to the Ragdale Foundation.

Kind words in support of my application to Ragdale came from my former boss on the editorial pages of the St. Paul Pioneer Press, and from a former student who came to live with us and who is now a dear friend.

Thanks be to the late Ronald D. Clark and to Steve Brandt.

Between visits to Ragdale, neighbors saw my need for a quiet place where I could work undisturbed by the charming distractions of a busy life; they offered me their cabin to use as a hideaway. I wrote; Jack came along to remind me to eat.

Thanks be to Jim Kalb and his late wife, Shirley.

When I had nearly finished writing, and knew no more than does a rutabaga about getting published, a cherished friend took me in hand and saw me through the process. This was a gift of ideas and of many, many hours.

Thanks be to Lynda McDonnell.

Any number of times, my computer gave me fits (you don't want to know). I am in computer kindergarten, helpless if things go wrong. To the rescue at a gallop came a whiz of a keyboard doctor.

Thanks be to Randy Eskenazi.

Special encouragement along the way came from special people.

Thanks be to Lorie and Jerry Pedersen, and to Pam Girod.

Finally, carloads of friends kept asking me how much longer it would be before they could finally read the book.

For the nudges, thanks be to the friends.